Things will never be the same

— *or will they?*

Greg Whateley, Andrew West and
Ashok Chanda

(With a foreword by Angus Hooke)

Table of Contents

SECTION 2 – THE RESPONSE

Foreword

In the middle of the 20th century, most people were largely unaware of the changes that were occurring in the world around them and of the impacts these changes would have on the way people lived, worked, and played. My father, with vivid memories of the then-recent Great Depression, told me many times "Your grandfather was a successful dairy farmer, I am a successful dairy farmer, and if you want to be successful in life you must also be a dairy farmer." My aunt – his sister – was a broader thinker. She assured me "You don't have to be a dairy farmer; there will always be a need for people to work on the railway lines and deliver the mail." At that time, this view of a constant work environment was accompanied by a feeling that crises were interruptions to normal life and not facilitators of major changes to what constitutes a normal life. When saying grace before meals my mother would pray that World War II would be over soon "so life can return to normal". We never questioned her thinking.

Both the world and our understanding of it have progressed. By the 1970s, many people were aware that significant change was occurring and that it would probably continue. However, because the ability to think in exponential terms had not provided any evolutionary benefits to humans during the three million years since Homo habilis first roamed the forests of central Africa, this change was implicitly viewed as linear. That we were coping reasonably well with change at the time was therefore accepted as strong evidence that we would continue to do so in the future.

Today, however, due largely to the global penetration of computers, mobile phones, and throw-away consumer durables, there is increasing recognition that much change, particularly where technology is involved, is exponential. Combined with the likelihood that we are approaching the kink of several technology curves, this suggests a real danger that the pace of change may soon make the early 2020s seem like a period of stability and tranquillity. In addition, the aftermath of unexpected events such as the oil price shocks in the 1970s and early 1980s and the Global Financial Crisis (GFC) in 2007-09 have demonstrated that the adjustments needed to cope with crises can speed up significantly the arrival and embedding of more permanent change.

With a future characterised by exponential change, technology kinks, and crises that serve as vehicles for fast-forwarding the impacts of change, it is fortuitous that a group of genuine experts with wide and deep backgrounds in education, music, and other industries has written about their experience during the COVID-19 crisis, including the immediate adjustments they were required to make, the division of those adjustments into ones that are transitory and should disappear when the crisis is over and others that will likely be more permanent, and lessons that can be learned from the crisis to make us be better prepared to meet the challenges and take advantage of the opportunities that will be presented by future crises.

The lead author, Emeritus Professor Greg Whateley, in his role of Deputy-Vice Chancellor of UBSS, has walked the talk on crises and effective adjustment to them. When the higher education sector in Sydney was required to move wholly to online delivery in March 2020, Greg led a team that, within a very short time frame, managed the construction of purpose-built online teaching studios, installation of state-of-the art communications equipment, and provision of tailored training for all UBSS staff involved in the new mode of delivery. Thus, while other higher education providers in Sydney were facing declining student satisfaction and a strong desire by students to return to face-to-face learning as soon as possible, UBSS students were reporting increasingly higher satisfaction rates with online delivery. In fact, after a year of online delivery, more that 90% of both undergraduate and postgraduate students expressed a preference to remain online indefinitely. Some authors of this book also achieved successful outcomes in the very challenging music industry, and they have been generous in making available the lessons they have learned.

This book provides valuable insights into crisis management, including the importance of prior planning, how to differentiate between temporary and more permanent changes, how to mobilise and train resources quickly, and how to implement new strategies effectively during a period of turmoil. It is essential reading for decision-makers, especially in the education and music industries, but also in other industries that are likely to face rapid change in the future.

Emeritus Professor Angus Hooke,

UBSS Centre for Scholarship and Research

Preface

This publication began with three stimulus papers – *Things will never be the same – or will they?* (Whateley), *COVID19 – The accelerator that evenly distributed the future* (West) and *Delivering change when things are constantly changing* (Chanda). The three papers (now Section 1 of this book) in turn were presented to selected authors both national and international for consideration and response.

Nineteen responses were received and are used as the additional chapters (now Section 2 of this book) and provide a valuable insight into the impact of COVID-19 on current practices in a diverse range of higher education (and allied) settings and foci. The chapters also represent projections on what the future of delivery and management in the sector will look like going forward.

Shawn Kok (Chapter 4) relates the issues and pressures in teaching pop music to students in China via a virtual environment.

Anurag Kanwar (Chapter 5) acknowledges COVID-19 as a global disruptor and focuses on the impact on Board meetings – suggesting they will never be the same.

Tom O'Connor (Chapter 6) explores the immediate and longer term similarities that COVID-19 has had highlighting some rather perturbing historical overtones.

Greg Whateley and Dimitri Kopanakis (Chapter 7) explore the renewed necessity of continuing professional development in order to keep up with rapid change with particular reference to the world of pharmacy.

Stephen Parker (Chapter 8) makes sense of the so called 'great resignation' and its impact on the 'great outsource' and the 'great automation'.

Lauren Whateley (Chapter 9) provides focus of the social impacts of COVID-19 and how things have returned to what could be seen as the 'new' normal.

Cyril Jankoff (Chapter 10) writes about the overall impacts on business life and explores what will return to normal and what will never change.

Daniel Bendel (Chapter 11) provides a valuable insight into the volatility of business at present and how to best cope.

Art Phillips (Chapter 12) explores the impact of the pandemic on a music business that required considerable innovation and flexibility – not to mention 'thinking outside of the box' to survive and grow.

Bruce Everett (Chapter 13) speaks from the heart on matters of forgiveness in difficult times and the essential ingredient to survival and renewal – optimism.

Eugene Seow (Chapter 14) explores the focus on live streamed concerts as an example of 'embracing the new normal'.

Ailsa Page (Chapter 15) reflects on what has actually changed – and what has changed 'forever'.

Fabian Lim (Chapter 16) considers the issues associated with being a musician in this time of change – and the significance of the meta-verse.

Ian Bofinger (Chapter 17) likens the ongoing disruptions in Higher Education to what he refers to as 'Groundhog Year'.

Om Huvanandana (Chapter 18) takes a look at the global economy and using Indonesia, Thailand, Vietnam and Singapore as useful considerations.

Richard Xi (Chapter 19) explores the importance and appropriateness of hybrid learning in the post COVID-19 environment.

Tom O'Connor (Chapter 20) uses the example of a 'timetable' as evidence that certain things will stay the same.

Andy Wong (Chapter 21) reflects on the need to manage' speed of change' as we navigate our way through the post pandemic period.

Jamie Rigg and Ian Bofinger (Chapter 22) provide a framework for a decimated live music industry to find a road to recovery.

The authors wish to thank sincerely the responders for their invaluable insights and the fact that all chapters were produced within a very short timeframe – in an effort to maintain currency. The speed has ensured the relevance of the issues considered. We would also like to take the opportunity of thanking **Veronica Sorace**, **Angus Hooke** and **Stephen Parker** for their efforts and support in the production process.

Our view is that things will never be the same – and this may not necessarily be a bad outcome.

Greg Whateley, Andrew West, Ashok Chanda
UBSS Centre for Scholarship and Research, March 2022

Section 1:

The Stimulus Papers

Chapter

1

Things will never be the same – or will they?

Greg Whateley

INTRODUCTION

Growing up in 1960s Melbourne (I was born in 1954), I was given my first real administration position at my primary school as 'milk monitor'. It came with significant responsibility, that of ensuring the milk bottles were brought in from the sun each morning in time for recess each day. The position came complete with a badge of honour, rubber gloves and a face mask - after all, I was opening milk bottles and placing straws down the neck of each, so hygiene was paramount. (Ironically, in Melbourne today - and throughout 2020 and 2021 - I have to wear a mask to collect my milk in the morning, but this is an aside.)

In those days, milk came in essentially one form - pasteurised - and later, homogenised. By the 1980s, a milk revolution took place. The 'Big M' arrived, providing flavoured milk, followed closely by a range of milk types. Today, we have a huge range of milk products catering to every possible need. The slogan accompanying the Big M revolution was, *'Things will never be the same now the Big M's here'*. And true enough, it has never been the same – arguably, for the better.

The same could be said of the 'big C' - COVID-19, because higher education will never be the same. I believe there will be a number of key impacts over the next, say, five years. Beyond that, who knows, we may simply resort to our old ways, though I think that is highly unlikely. The anticipated short-term changes, though, are laid out, accordingly.

HEIGHTENED SENSE OF HYGIENE

It is self-evident that sanitisation stations, face masks, heightened cleaning regimes, social distancing protocols and general hygiene awareness are the new norm. Institutions (such as mine) will flock towards COVID-safe certification. Yes, it adds additional cost and red tape. But, in truth, better hygiene standards can only be a good thing. The demands of the certification ensure that the appropriate level of attention to hygiene related matters is embedded within the organisation.

Hopefully, post-pandemic, we will see fewer flus and colds on campus - and the associated disruptions - as students and staff remain more conscious of the importance of hygiene and the simple act of washing their hands regularly throughout the day. Heightened hygiene has certainly been a feature of the last two years - in particular - and will probably remain a high-profile activity moving forward.

What will become the norm is students and staff not coming on to campus if they are unwell. The temptation to 'soldier on' is a thing of the past. If you are unwell, taking the time out and recovering at home will be the more common practice. This will have an impact on contractual arrangements, in terms of annual sick leave allowances, but as it becomes the norm, legislation will follow. The standard 10-day allowance will probably not do the trick anymore - time will tell.

CHANGES TO ASSESSMENT AND FEEDBACK

The inevitable concern about online examination security will lead to a fundamental rethink of the balance of exams versus assignments. The trend is towards a 60:40 model. My institution, like many, has already adjusted the examination regime we had in place pre-COVID. Our pre-COVID model was an examination regime (Weeks 5, 9 and 13/14) - this has now been replaced by 60% assignment focus and a final examination of 40%. Partial mandatory examinations satisfy accreditation requirements from groups like CPA, CAANZ and IPA.

Further, the importance of feedback to students will be emphasised. Zaglas (2020) recently highlighted the importance of feedback in the digital environment, and educators will need to bridge the tyranny of distance with more proactive feedback to students learning remotely.

Generally speaking, teaching staff have been good at this, however, the new digital focus necessitates new feedback strategies. My own institution consistently scores well with students in the domain of feedback, as evidenced in the ongoing Student Feedback on Units (**SFUs**), but further focus and attention will become the norm.

CHANGES TO WAYS OF WORKING AND COMMUNICATING FOR PROFESSIONAL STAFF

The relocation of professional staff to a work-from-home environment has had both positive and negative outcomes to date. Less efficient organisations have further suffered; the more nimble and productive ones have actually transitioned well. My own institution was quick to allow professional staff added flexibility - on the other hand, it mandated on-campus online delivery for academic staff to ensure presentation standards were maintained.

As Kidd (2020) argues, "COVID-19 has forever changed the way that many people work. Businesses have had to quickly move to models that allow work to be performed remotely and with increased flexibility." There is little surprise here.

While much has been said of the shift to online for teachers, I think it is non-teaching roles that will most acutely embrace remote working post-pandemic. Routine tasks are easily enough managed. Meetings have become considerably more efficient and focussed online. Research, scholarship, and projects have also been effectively managed online, as has working remotely.

We have found a work-from-home (**WFH**) roster for professional staff works well and that there is minimal disruption. Whether staff wish to return to campus is uncertain. I suspect the most likely outcome will be a mix of WFH and onsite - if I were to take a stab, I would suggest 3 days offsite, and 2 days onsite will become a regular pattern.

INCREASED USE OF TECHNOLOGY

Embracing technology would always have occurred, regardless of COVID-19, however, it is the types of technology that have been, and will continue to be, embraced by the higher education sector that will fundamentally change.

Whether or not full classes return to onsite lecture theatres, there will now be a blended approach to teaching and learning. The flipped classroom certainly gathered some momentum during the last few years, but a truly balanced approach is now inevitable. The current lingo around this is the 'hybrid' mode (Whateley, 2021) - that is, all sessions are available online with limited access to classrooms in a safe and responsible way. The student decides (in effect) to study online or F2F - and the institution will provide both options simultaneously.

Interestingly, students appear to prefer such an approach. A recent survey of our students found that 92 per cent would prefer classes to stay online. There is likely a combination of factors driving this, including reduced commuting time and cost, convenience, effective use of technology, as well as perhaps an alleviation of the fear of asking questions in a full lecture theatre.

The hybrid modelling is the most likely outcome, especially for business schools. Understandably, there will be a call for F2F practical classes that are difficult to simulate online, but I suspect the growth of online theory classes will remain strong and dominant moving forward.

OBSESSION WITH ACADEMIC INTEGRITY AND USE OF PROCTORING INVIGILATION SOFTWARE

Regulators will become obsessed (if not already) with academic integrity. This will flow onto administrators and managers. Good schools already have a solid system of integrity management.

While regulatory challenges have been with us for many years, they have become much more heightened in recent times as a result of concerns over 'digital fraud'. As such, expect the market for proctoring tools to expand noticeably, given the plethora of products available.

It is important to note the increased pressure and demands on professional staff who monitor and manage the online proctoring. With all new initiatives, it does take time and effort to embed change. It will come as no surprise to anyone that change is often accompanied by resistance, even though change is inevitable. The only constant, remember, is change!

CHANGE FOR THE BETTER

While we would all prefer the pandemic never happened, the change it has brought about is irrevocable. And, that change is not necessarily a bad thing either.

Higher education has needed a shake-up for some time; teaching and learning at universities has long needed a jolt. The current pandemic has challenged the different ways administrators and teachers alike go about their work. The relationship between cost and quality is being challenged online - and this may be a positive.

Post five years, there is an argument that COVID-19 will simply be a thing of the past - a memory - not unlike the Spanish Flu, Swine Flu, and Hong Kong Flu, and only time will tell. It may be deemed an historical event - a once in a lifetime scenario. For the moment, change is inevitable, and we can either embrace it or be left behind.

Emeritus Professor Greg Whateley, is currently Deputy Vice Chancellor, Group Colleges Australia

REFERENCES

Kidd, E. (2020) 'My staff don't want to return to work - coming back after COVID-19'. Human Resources Director, 12 May 2020

Whateley, G. (2021) 'What is meant by 'hybrid' delivery and how does it work in higher education'. Campus Review, 12 July 2021

Zaglas, W. (2020) 'Delivering quality feedback to students and staff with remote learning and skeleton staff'. Campus Review, 11 September 2020

Chapter

2

COVID-19 – The accelerator that evenly distributed the future

Andrew West

INTRODUCTION

One of my favourite authors, William Gibson, (1993) stated in a radio interview, "The future is already here. It's just not evenly distributed yet." Gibson is well credentialed to have an understanding of the future, and, among many other predictions, in his 1984 novel, 'Neuromancer', he predicted the arrival of the internet, writing about the globally interconnected computer network of data, the 'web' and 'cyberspace'. Gibson (1993) explained his quote about the future - that there are things that will be part of the normal and everyday lives for all in the future that already exist for some today, and that what will constitute change in the short and medium term is the spread from the some to the many. It is COVID-19, as the accelerator, that has hastened this spread.

Before COVID-19, there was a range of trends, both societal and technological, and it was uncertain when, how, or even if, they would impact us. Since early 2020, however, with COVID-19 as the great accelerator (Bradley et al, 2020), the future is somewhat clearer, in particular in the higher education sector. This paper will look at three trends that have become the norm in the post COVID-19 world: online delivery, hybrid work and higher education, and life-long learning qualifications. I will highlight some studies and observations in higher education, as well as outline some of the Australian government policy responses to this change in a post COVID-19 world.

ONLINE DELIVERY OF HIGHER EDUCATION

Online delivery in its many forms has existed for decades in higher education in Australia. Open Learning Australia first commenced in 1993 as a consortium of six universities led by the University of Melbourne (*https://www.open.edu.au/about-us*). There is a long history of innovation in Australian higher education to deliver learning, and widely. Over a century ago, 1911 saw the first instance of distance learning in Australia, with print-based education mailed to university students in the rural areas and regions (Gallagher, 2001). In 1951, the world's first 'school of the air' was opened in Alice Springs, where teachers used mailed printed material and radio to communicate with students. This innovation in Australian higher education continues today.

Online delivery in higher education was able to take its current form during the 3rd Industrial Revolution with the internet, memory and programmable computer networks (Schwab, 2017). This will further develop in this age of the 4th Industrial Revolution (**4th IR**), as education integrates automation, artificial intelligence, Internet of Things, virtual reality (**VR**) and robotics. The full extent of the integration of 4th IR technologies has not fully been realised yet. With the announcement of the change in name from Facebook to Meta, and the prioritisation of the metaverse being available in 2030, this has provided a future focal point for higher education. VR student experience provides the opportunity to bring back interaction, engagement, and rapport, often lost in the shift to the digital world. The possibilities are endless with virtual classrooms, meeting spaces and work integrated learning opportunities. Interestingly, in a recent study, students preferred VR hybrid to the standard classroom hybrid model (Hogan, 2021).

Furthermore, higher education has a role to play to ensure that the knowledge, skills, and attributes required by the 4th IR workforce are embedded in all courses delivered, in order that students are work-ready. Higher education also provides research across a range of disciplines to identify and provide insights into the impact of the 4th IR and the way in which it drives societal change.

COVID-19 has certainly accelerated the widespread use and acceptance of online higher education delivery. From March 2020, all higher education has been delivered online due to the COVID lockdowns. This has resulted in the acceptance - by students - of the benefits of online delivery. It may be said, the online delivery method is accepted by many as a positive change. "These developments have also occurred in a broader context of pedagogically-led reform of teaching and learning, shifting from teacher-centred learning to learner-centred, from classroom to flipped classroom, from low engagement to high engagement, and from delivering curriculum content to delivering roadmaps, frameworks and opportunities" (Sankey, 2021).

An Australasian Council on Open Distance and eLearning (**ACODE**) survey of all Australian universities in November 2020, and follow up surveys in 2021, found the following results -

- Only 32% of institutions expected to return to campus lectures in 2021.
- Even fewer (22%) said they would be returning to campus-based full lecturing beyond 2021, with 14% indicating they would not be returning to lectures at all, and a further 16% un-decided (Sankey, 2021).

This wider acceptance of online delivery is also confirmed by the UBSS student survey results, taken each trimester since the beginning of the pandemic in March 2020, with 92% of students preferring to remain with online delivery rather than on campus, face-to-face (**F2F**). It is the intention of UBSS to offer a hybrid model of online and F2F delivery into the future.

The move to online delivery is also a global phenomenon. With this comes the driver of change from the private sector, who, through Online Program Managers (**OPMs**), provides the digital innovation and content development to be 'White Labelled' and delivered under the name of the university, often using identical content across institutions, without the knowledge of the students (HolonIQ, 2021a). These OPMs provide the expertise, resources, and scale to provide cost effective student management to universities, faster and more specialised instructional design, and digital focussed student recruitment.

Australian examples include SEEK and Online Education Services, in partnership with Swinburne Online, Keypath International (*https://keypathedu.com.au/our-partners*), who recently listed on the Australian Stock Exchange, the partnership now extending to nine Australian universities: Deakin University, University of NSW, RMIT, James Cook University, Southern Cross University, Victoria University, Edith Cowan University, University of Technology Sydney and University of Canberra. Keypath also have 24 other university partnerships, globally. Other Australian companies in this space are Studiosity (*https://www.studiosity.com/*), a student experience and support platform, part owned by Online Education Services, and Curio (*https://curio.co/*), a learning design and digital tutor solution agency.

These local companies are minnows compared to the global privately backed OPMs of Edx, 2U, Noodle and Zovio, to name a few. These companies are listed in the USA, where the top 60 global OPMs are situated. The current OPM market in the USA is valued at USD3.9bn and is forecast to reach USD7.7bn by 2025. (HolonIQ , 2021a). The rapid speed of the signups to partnerships is staggering, with 450 partnership agreements signed in the first 6 months of 2021. All 40 Australian universities either have an OPM partner or are looking to establish a partnership by 2022 (West, 2021). The impact of COVID-19 on this industry is to increase compound annual growth rate from a high 13% per annum pre-COVID, to an eye-watering 18% in 2021 (HolonIQ, 2021b). Online delivery is definitely here to stay.

HYBRID MODEL WORKPLACE AND HIGHER EDUCATION DELIVERY

There has been conjecture about whether staff will return to the workplace post the COVID lockdowns. There is also discussion as to whether higher education will move to the hybrid, blended or online delivery model. This is explored by UBSS in our recent publication, "Exploring a new era – hybrid, blended and online learning" (Whateley, Chanda, West, 2021).

As Australia begins to open the international borders in early 2022, and international students return, there is a move to the hybrid, blended and online models. For the international student wishing to have an Australian education qualification, there is a move away from the on campus F2F model to online, offshore and from third party providers (TEQSA, 2021a). Even though the borders are currently open, the process of bringing in the 140,000 international students with study visas is expected to take us to mid-2022 (Universities Australia, 2021). This will mean, at least for the first half of 2022, international students and on campus in Australia students will need to be taught together, requiring either a hybrid or online model. Sydney University has announced the 'hyflex mode' of delivery, commencing in 2022 (Baker, 2021). Large lectures, for more than 120 students - about 10 per cent of classes - will mostly be held online, but students will be expected to attend smaller classes, such as tutorials, seminars, and practical activities, in person.

Even the higher education workplace is moving to a hybrid model, with many universities adjusting to staff requests to work from home and to the new workplace norms. Sydney University management has released a "flex work policy proposal" that allows continuing and fixed term staff to work from anywhere (**WFA**). The proposal suggests, "A hybrid model may combine the best aspects of remote work with the benefits of coming to campus for collaboration, team-building, and non-remote tasks" (Baker, 2021).

This change impacts on the work environment, freeing up workspace previously used as offices. In both Sydney University and Melbourne University, it is expected there will be some enclosed offices, but most workspaces will be open space with an area for staff learning materials and storage. Swinburne University and RMIT will also continue with flexible working arrangements. Once these measures are put in place for the delivery of higher education learning and for the higher education workplace, the learning environment as we knew it will likely not return, as the drivers of societal normalisation and further technology development will take us further down the hybrid path.

FUTURE OF WORK – MORE WORK INTEGRATED LEARNING AND LIFE-LONG LEARNING

Another trend in higher education that has been accelerated by COVID-19 is the student demand for qualifications, and alongside this demand, the changed requirements of the labour force of the future. The recently published, 'University-industry Collaboration in Teaching and Learning', authored by Emeritus Professor Martin Bean and Emeritus Professor Peter Dawkins, observes that "digital technology and skills are vital to the future of our economy and to the successful movement between industry and the tertiary education sectors, ensuring all Australians can access opportunities for skilled, productive work, and contribute to the solutions and services needed in the decade ahead" (Bean and Dawkins, 2021, page 10).

The report found that the latest employment projections from the National Skills Commission demonstrate how critical a combination of knowledge, skills, connections, and direct working experience will be to the future performance of the Australian economy. The 7 short-term recommendations are defined as such:

1. National skills taxonomy developed
2. Implement Australian Quality Framework reform building on the Noonan Report (Noonan P, 2019)
3. Create a Unified Credentials Platform
4. Industry-focused micro-credentials
5. National cadetships
6. Learning outcomes and work-integrated learning
7. Cross-sectoral partnerships between universities, industry, and government

There are opportunities to develop the in-demand, industry-relevant experiences and working knowledge that together build the capability of learners to be successful in the workplace and develop the connections and mindsets that improve their earnings and opportunities over their lifetime.

The Australian government has pursued this agenda to a certain extent, with a focus on university and industry partnerships, commercialisation of research, and more micro credentialling - this includes the Undergraduate Certificate introduced in 2020, to continue to mid-2025, at least (TEQSA, 2021b). This is one step towards making more flexible changes to the AQF (Australian Qualifications Framework Addendum No.3). The current AQF was introduced in 1995 to "underpin the national system of qualifications in Australia, encompassing higher education, vocational education and training and schools" (*www.aqf.edu.au*). Whether the Australian government continues on this path of reform to the AQF is to be seen, as is the shape Australian qualifications will take.

A blueprint for these reforms has been proposed by the Expert Panel for the Review of the Australian Qualifications Framework (**AQF**), chaired by Professor Peter Noonan, and released in 2019 (Noonan, 2019). The report recognised that many jobs today would become redundant in the near future, namely, the roles that are standardised, as well as the routine production and service delivery roles. The new jobs to replace them will focus on human aptitudes and capabilities, in particular those roles which have the capacity to incorporate and work alongside technology. The report recognised in 2019 that workplaces were becoming more flexible and diverse in employment and work practices - that they are less hierarchical, with a premium put on teamwork, collaboration, the collective, rather than individual achievements (Noonan, 2019). As such, all workplaces need to be developed and recognised within the current qualification framework. Some of the recommendations of the proposed new AQF would be to work towards more flexibility, rather than the hierarchical 10 levels, have a common taxonomy and recognise stackable learning of micro-credentials, with a focus more on applied skills as well as knowledge (Noonan, 2019 page 9-11). The implementation of the process to incorporate these AQF changes lies with the Council of Australian Governments (**COAG**) Education Council and the COAG Skills Council.

There is mounting external pressure for reform as far as the AQF, the higher education categories and other structures of the Australian higher education sector are concerned. Where the impacts of globalisation may have slowed in many sectors across the world, its full impact is still to be felt in higher education. COVID-19 has restricted mobility for workers and students for a period of two years, but the pent-up demand for individuals and their families to make a better life for themselves is even stronger, and with that, the move across the globe. The movement of people may have been impacted by COVID-19, but data, technologies and flow of ideas has increased. These are all enablers of further digital disruption of OPMs, Massive Online Open Colleges (**MOOCs**), micro-credentials, and non-accredited continuing education.

There is a growth in the demand for what is termed a 'non-award' qualification under the Australian national AQF. The student may choose an internationally recognised certification from Google, Amazon, LinkedIn Learning or EdX. Furthermore, the decision process for future study may be between an Australian university qualification within the tightly regulated AQF or an internationally recognised corporate brand offering a certification. The full impact of the OPMs and other multi-national technology companies has not been felt in Australia yet, but the technological and societal conditions are in place for this to occur.

COVID-19 has impacted all of us in so many ways. COVID-19 has acted as the accelerator to many long-term trends that were expected to have an impact on the higher education sector over the coming decades into the here and now. These changes are likely to remain. The question still beckons… what are the other futures that are already here, that are yet to be distributed?

Professor Andrew West, is currently Dean, Universal Business School Sydney

REFERENCES

Baker J (2021) Sydney University pursues hybrid model of online and in-person classes, December 1, 2021. *https://www.smh.com.au/national/nsw/sydney-university-pursues-hybrid-model-of-online-and-in-person-classes-20211201-p59duj.html*, viewed December 10, 2021.

Bean M and Dawkins P (2021) Review of University-Industry Collaboration in Teaching and Learning. *https://www.dese.gov.au/higher-education-reviews-and-consultations/resources/universityindustry-collaboration-teaching-and-learning-review*

Bradley C, Hirt M, Hudson S, Northcote N and Smit S (2020) The Great Acceleration. *https://www.mckinsey.com/business-functions/strategy-and-corporate-finance/our-insights/the-great-acceleration*, viewed April 2, 2021.

Gallagher M (2001) E- Learning in Post-Secondary Education: Trends, Issues and Policy Challenges Ahead, 7th OECD/Japan Seminar, June 5 and 6, 2001.

Gibson W (1984) Neuromancer, Ace, New York, USA.

Gibson W (1993) Fresh Air Radio Interview, National Public Radio (August 31, 1993).

Hogan S (2021) Virtual reality a "positive impact" on hybrid learning, posted on Nov 11, 2021. *https://thepienews.com/news/vr-positive-impact-hybrid-model-learning/*, viewed December 15, 2021.

HolonIQ (2021a) 244 University Partnerships in the First Half of 2021. *https://www.holoniq.com/notes/opm-mooc-opx.-244-university-partnerships-in-the-first-half-of-2021/*, viewed September 24, 2021.

Holon IQ (2021b) 109 New OPM Bootcamp and Pathways Partnerships in Q1, 2021. *https://www.holoniq.com/notes/100-new-opm-bootcamp-and-pathway-partnerships-in-q1-2021/*, viewed December 10, 2021.

Noonan P (2019) Review of the Australian Qualifications Framework Final Report 2019. *https://www.dese.gov.au/download/4707/review-australian-qualifications-framework-final-report-2019/18863/document/pdf*, viewed May 10, 2021.

Sankey M (2021) Australasian Council on Open, Distance and eLearning (ACODE), Returning to lectures in 2021. *https://www.acode.edu.au/pluginfile.php/9235/mod_resource/content/7/white%20paper.pdf*

Schwab K (2017) The Fourth Industrial Revolution, Penguin UK, Great Britain.

TEQSA (2021b) Forward impact of COVID-19 on Australian higher education. *https://www.teqsa.gov.au/latest-news/publications/forward-impact-covid-19-australian-higher-education-report*, viewed December 15, 2021.

TEQSA (2021b) Undergraduate Certificates Continue until Mid-2025. *https://www.teqsa.gov.au/latest-news/articles/undergraduate-certificates-continue-until-mid-2025*, viewed December 15, 2021.

Universities Australia (2021) Australia's Migration Program 2022-2023. *https://www.universitiesaustralia.edu.au/wp-content/uploads/2021/12/211213-Australias-Migration-Program-2022-2023-Submission.pdf*

West A and Whateley G (2021) 'The fourth industrial age is here for higher education to embrace' was published on Monday, May 10 in Campus Review.

West A (2021) OPM is not just another TLA, Chapter 14, Updating and enhancing unit content, delivery, and assessment (Hooke and Whateley). *https://www.ubss.edu.au/articles/2021/october/opm-is-not-just-another-tla/*

Whateley G., West A. and Chanda A (2021) Exploring a new era – hybrid, blended and online learning. Smart Questions, ISBN 978-1-907453-31-1.

Chapter

3

Delivering Change When Things are Constantly Changing

Ashok Chanda

INTRODUCTION

In the 1990s when I was graduating, a highly popular buzz term - 'change management' - could be heard on every corner. We were obsessed with this term and each one of us was trying to make sense of, and give meaning to, this terminology. A number of high-profile books emerged on the subject, including those written by (Conner, 1993), (Jick, 1993), (LaMarsh, 1995), (Kotter, 1996) and (Johnson, 1999), together providing deep insights in to how to manage change, in general, as well as, more specifically, in the context of an organisation. Among these, 'Who Moved My Cheese?' (Johnson, 1999) was my favourite, as it was simple, and easy to digest - indeed, I considered the book an exemplary work. I used the 'Mouse Story' extensively during my corporate and academic engagements to emphasise that 'change is constant' and 'acceptance of the change is the way of life'.

When there is a 'change', there is always a 'resistance to change', much like Newton's second law of physics. For me, change and resistance go hand in hand. A classic example of change management occurred when information technology began to revolutionise business - in fact, our lives as well. It was hard for all of us to digest just how computerisation would take over human tasks, and we believed that people would end up jobless. That was not the case, however, and eventually we became obsessed with computers more than we resisted the entry of computers into our lives. Today, technologies feature in our lives and we have happily accepted this change.

That another big change in our lives came along, cannot go unsaid - the COVID-19 pandemic. The impact of the pandemic has seen our lives change enormously - everything, from our shopping habits, travel, hospitality and social activities, to sport, working arrangements, education delivery and even the health system, has undergone dramatic transformation.

The education sector has witnessed a most significant change in the way that the imparting of knowledge has shifted from face-to-face to online delivery (OECD, 2020). COVID-19 lockdowns have meant deserted city streets, and the campuses of universities and institutions, abandoned. Students are no longer attending lectures by being physically present, but rather, taking lectures remotely, and lecturers (in some cases) are delivering lectures from their home office. Initially, this approach was met with resistance, with institutions - their staff, lecturers, and students alike - struggling to accept the change. As we enter 2022, however, we are witness to the fact that this change has slowly become the new way of life in the education sector. How this has become possible, alongside what has inspired institutions, lecturers, and students to make this change, is worth examining. In this paper, I take a close look at how education delivery is, indeed, defined by change, as those responsible for this delivery not only continue to respond to the constant changes surrounding the education sector, but essentially, begin to embrace the changes within the sector.

WHAT HAS CHANGED IN THE EDUCATION SYSTEM DUE TO COVID-19?

Within the education system, there have been many changes due to COVID-19. While taking a close look at what really has changed, the following (though not exhaustive), is well worth considering.

- FROM believing that education can only be delivered face-to-face in the presence of a teacher and students, TO education can also be delivered without being present, that is, face-to-face, and can be delivered online as effectively.

- FROM maintaining admissions and enrolments in specific locations, where students had to move physically, TO enrolling in any institution without physically relocating.

- FROM establishing mammoth size campuses and infrastructure, housing lecture theatres, classrooms, faculty areas, cafeterias, the ideologies, TO having a small home office and virtual classrooms, with suitable digitally equipped tech-rooms.

- FROM lecturers physically present in classrooms and using power points and slides to deliver their lectures, TO lecturers learning how to deliver webinars and tutorials and sessions, using technology and software from remote locations.

- FROM building dependency on physical hardbound prescribed textbooks which students carry around all year, TO moving to digital content and e-books, using iPads, laptops, and mobile devices.

- FROM procuring and housing large volumes of hardbound books, magazines, and periodicals in library setups, TO online library and electronic databases, making it easy to search and research.

- FROM students making appointments to meet lecturers or student support staff in person, TO an online chat and virtual appointment environment, where students do not physically queue-up.

- FROM physical classroom-based invigilated examinations, TO online assessments, proctored exams which students can attempt from any location.

- FROM showing up at the workstation to manage day-to-day tasks, TO working from home and continuing to do the work as usual.

- FROM students lining up at the notice board to take a glimpse of the marks and information on the timetable and to view class arrangements, TO mobile apps delivering all necessary information relating to the institute, timetables, assessments, grades, and even subject enrolment, campus navigation, and so on.

We know that accepting such changes - from lecturers and students tuning in to one set of processes and now having to trust a new way of education delivery - is a challenge, and that it takes great effort and often a long time. With the COVID-19 situation, however, change is occurring at an accelerated pace, and it seems there is no way of escaping the change; instead, we may find that if we do not embrace the change, the alternative is to 'go out of business'.

HOW IS CHANGE ADOPTED IN EDUCATION DELIVERY AND LEARNING?

Our reaction to change is always influenced by its nature. When a change is purely of a technical nature, such as a new machine or an altered component, then the expectation is that existing knowledge be applied in a mechanistic manner. When the change is unexpected and non-technical in nature, however, people orientation plays an important role. To simplify this connotation, we have created the Change Matrix (see Figure 1) which depicts how changes are shaping up in the education sector.

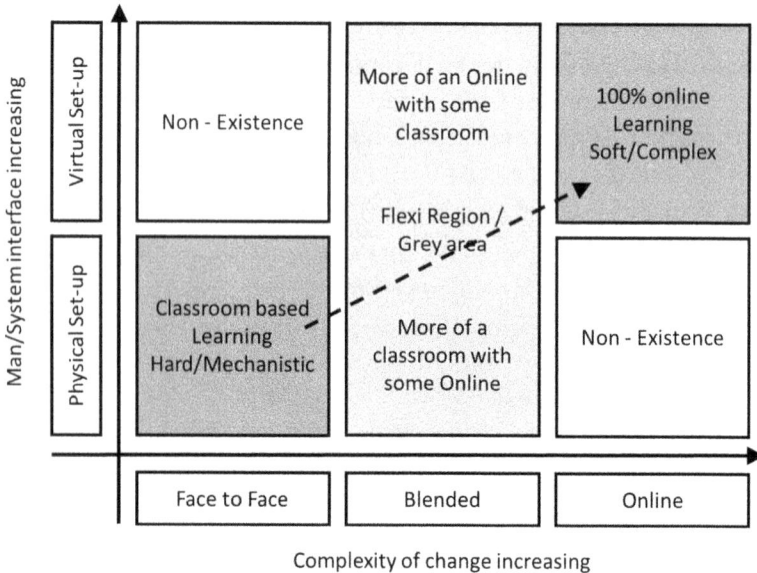

Figure 1 - Change Matrix (in the context of learning)

The Change Matrix represents how mankind and system interface increases with an increase in the complexity of a changed delivery in education and learning. A hard or mechanistic change exists towards the left-hand side of the spectrum. Actually, it is a reasonably static change environment - clearly quantifiable, with immediate implications and minimum mankind/system interface. At the extreme soft end of the spectrum, objectives and time scale become unclear and highly dynamic. Issues that typically surface involve individual and group interface.

Hard/mechanistic change has clear and concise definitions, while soft/complex changes are difficult to define. Hard changes are mostly technical in nature, while soft changes are predominantly interpersonal and in social terms. Delivering change in the soft and complex environment demands involvement and constant learning.

To articulate the above in the real-life situation, two examples are described below.

From training centre to virtual training – Gati Ltd, a large logistics organisation

Gati is a pioneer in express distribution, a company in India, which operates through hundreds of offices and depots across length and breadth of country. Training of employees involves bringing personnel together in different groups at various training centres - and this has always been a significant challenge. Introduced, in 2000, was a new approach to learning, using video cameras and microphones, set up at six training centres in order to connect, simultaneously, with employees attending training. This was a new experiment of imparting training in a virtual set-up without travelling to one, single location. The acceptance of such a method of training was a challenge from the outset - but eventually, it worked very well.

From classroom delivery to online delivery – UBSS, a higher education provider

UBSS, an Australian higher education provider, until 2018, delivered education only via classrooms within its Sydney CBD campus. Students attended class and lecturers delivered the courses as scheduled, face-to-face. With the government mandate of shutting down campuses due to health precautions, UBSS moved to online delivery. With significant investment in setting up an infrastructure for online delivery, faculty were asked to deliver sessions online, using a classroom, studio style, but without students attending physically. Initially, this arrangement was not welcomed by some, but slowly, and with persistence (and significant staff training), the changes were accepted. Today, UBSS can claim education is delivered 100% online.

HOW TO LIVE WITH THE CHANGE? CONCEPT OF 'LEARNING INSTITUTIONS'

It would be erroneous when discussing delivery change to not consider the concept of the 'learning organisation'. This term has become increasingly popular among management gurus and leaders of change - attributed by Peter Senge in his epic book, 'The Fifth Discipline' (Senge, 1990). In the current situation, where the institutions are embracing change, the appropriateness of the term seems to be magnified when we consider the concept of *learning institutions*. A lesson from Senge, then…we may well build *learning organisations* and *learning institutions* in the same vein - following five disciplines.

Build a shared vision

As far as learning institutions are concerned, the vision is created through interaction and discussion with the academics and students. Many institutions' leaders have personal visions that lack the qualities to transfer to a shared vision. The only way to create a shared vision is by balancing an institution's vision with that of the individual. Leadership, academics, and a student community who do not share the same vision might not contribute as much to the institution.

Develop systems thinking

Instead of focusing on individual issues, systems thinking reflects the observational process of an entire system. An institution's leadership and academics need to understand that every action and consequence is interconnected. Online delivery requires a cohesive process from all associated. Academic focus on individual subjects is common and, therefore, the notion of 'seeing the big picture' is often overlooked. When the correlation is understood, it enables us to see interrelationships and patterns of change.

Create mental models

Leadership and academics must identify the values of the institution. A correct understanding of who we are will enable us to visualise where to go and how to develop further. The institution has to be flexible in accepting change, new mental models, and a new image of the institution itself. The most successful institutions may well be those whose members can learn and adapt to new models sooner than their competitors.

Drive team-learning

To accomplish excellent functional team dynamics, team-learning is of primary importance, and it is the means by which personal mastery and shared vision are brought together. It is crucial for the institution's leadership and academics to work as a team. The first step is to set up dialogue when change is on the horizon.

Celebrate personal mastery

Personal mastery occurs when an individual has a clear vision of a goal, combined with an accurate perception of reality. The creative tension depends on a clear understanding of current reality. For this reason, for personal mastery and the related discipline of a shared vision, looking at and sharing the truth is crucial. Some academics, however, may believe they lack the competencies to drive online delivery as they are not familiar with current pedagogy, or are absorbed in old school thinking. In such situations, training is the best solution if one is to build competency and confidence.

CONCLUSION

As we enter the COVID-19 recovery phase, it will be critical to reflect on the changes that have occurred within our educational system. Disruptions on the scale we have just witnessed are not limited to pandemics, but may also occur as a result of natural, political, economic and environmental disorder. Our capacity to react effectively and efficiently in the future will hinge on our foresight, our flexibility, and our preparedness for change.

Real change often takes place in deep crises, and, as such, this moment in time holds the very real possibility that we will not return to the status quo when things return to "normal". While this current crisis has had, and continues to have, deeply disruptive implications, including for education, not all disruptions in the long run will be deemed negative, even if we have been taken by surprise and challenged by not having predetermined outcomes. It will be the nature of our collective and systemic response to these disruptions that will determine how we are affected by them.

Associate Professor Ashok Chanda, is currently Provost, UBSS Online Campus, Group Colleges Australia

REFERENCES

Conner. (1993). Managing At the Speed of Change. Random House. Retrieved from *https://www.amazon.com/Managing-Speed-Change-Daryl-Conner/dp/0679406840*

Jick. (1993). Managing Change: Cases and Concepts: Text and Cases. McGraw-Hill. Retrieved from *https://www.amazon.com.au/Managing-Change-Cases-Concepts-Text/dp/0073102741*

Johnson. (1999). Who Moved My Cheese. Vermilion. Retrieved from *https://www.amazon.com.au/Moved-Cheese-Spencer-M-D-Johnson/dp/0091816971/*

Kotter. (1996). Leading Change. Harvard Business Review Press. Retrieved from *https://www.amazon.com.au/Leading-Change-New-Preface-Author/dp/1422186431*

LaMarsh. (1995). Changing the Way We Change. Prentice Hall. Retrieved from *https://www.amazon.com.au/Changing-Way-Change-Jeanenne-Lamarsh/dp/0201633647*

OECD. (2020). The Impact Of Covid-19 On Education Insights From Education At A Glance 2020. Retrieved from *https://www.oecd.org/education/the-impact-of-covid-19-on-education-insights-education-at-a-glance-2020.pdf*

Senge, P. (1990). The Fifth Discipline: The Art & Practice of The Learning Organization. Crown. Retrieved from *https://www.amazon.com.au/Fifth-Discipline-Practice-Learning-Organization/dp/0385517254/*

Section 2:

The Response Papers

Chapter

4

Methodolatry: Pedagogical issues in Teaching Pop Music to China Students in Virtual Environments

Shawn Kok

INTRODUCTION

"Critical" consideration of curriculum theory is missing when it comes to the preparation of most music teachers today. Instead, "methods and materials" courses typically stress the "how-to" delivery of pre-packaged, teacher-proof teaching materials, such as, basal song series and instrumental methods books; or courses are delivered under the auspices of what I have called "methodolatry" (Regelski, 2005).

CONTEXTUALISING THE PRACTICE

Music educators have an increasingly arduous task of empowering students with knowledge, specific skills, and passion in an increasingly globalised world, especially when encountering intersections where conventional art forms, disciplines, and mediums converge and probe into one another, such as with video and traditional music performance. This curriculum was designed for China music university students who take a semester-long online module called Virtual Live Music Performance, through Lasalle College of the Arts, a higher education arts institution in Singapore. Developed with a praxial philosophy at its core, I replaced "methods and materials" with critical considerations for the latest mainstream musical trends, digital technologies, and industry standards, under the auspices of what Thomas A. Regelski calls "methodolatry" (2002), emerging literature on online learning, and the Constructivist Learning Theory (Hein, 1991). The intention of this curriculum is to present a syllabus that is realistic, reflective of current popular music practices, and capable of transiting learners effectively from vocation to livelihood.

VIRTUAL LIVE MUSIC PERFORMANCE

The aim of this semester-long module is threefold:

- To cultivate an understanding of virtual music performance
- To equip learners with knowledge and skills in performing music for camera
- To enable learners to discover their identity within the musical contexts of their choice.

Learners explore performing for the camera, that is, the practice of performing music in a virtual space and the specific kinds of skills required to do so effectively. Students examine the uses of multimedia equipment and digital technologies, technology-infused performances, and design a series of technology-based performances and implement them in real-world scenarios, using broadcast software and applications, social media platforms, mobile applications, or computer software.

RATIONALE FOR THE ONLINE CURRICULUM

The 2019 Covid pandemic quickened the migration of music making and consumption from face-to-face to the internet, and exponentially changed the way music is performed, communicated, and consumed in a globalised context, for both music performers and audiences (Taylor, 2020). Largely, four common formats of music performance have emerged. The first is a direct live broadcast or live stream, from the mobile phone or desktop, with the use of a digital application or software. The second format is like the first, but instead of performing solo, the performer gets to "join broadcast", or otherwise colloquially known as "PK" or "Player Kill" with another user, on the same social media network or digital platform. The third format takes the first format to a grander scale, likened to an actual music concert, but instead of being live, performances are pre-recorded and played back during stipulated "performance times". The fourth format is like the third, but entirely live. Many musical artists across the globe are following suit. Because of this shift, I had to adjust the curriculum if I wanted to be prudent, remain applicable, and produce relevant future music practitioners and educators for the industries - as underscored by Jones (2007). This semester-long module, "Live Ensemble", which had always been conducted in-person before the pandemic had to be modified into a completely online module.

CRITICAL PEDAGOGY AND A CULTURALLY RESPONSIVE CURRICULUM

To be culturally responsive in one's teaching means to be starkly aware that for knowledge and skills to be created and transmitted, they must be positioned within the experiences and perspectives of the students, as what is closer to the heart carries more meaning and appeal, allowing for better and more effective learning (Gay, 2000). The demography of the Chinese students I was teaching was significantly more diverse than my Lasalle (Singapore) students. Comprising of undergraduate music students from music conservatories and adjacent disciplines, such as, music production and audio production, working musicians and music teachers, and mature students from disciplines outside of music, they form a complex and uneven palette of musical perspectives and lived experiences, with little common factors apart from their working language and constant engagement with music. In referencing Gay (2002), a culturally responsive educator strives to:

- Create an evolving understanding about ethnic and cultural diversity inside and outside the curriculum
- Build communities through constant interaction with, and caring for, diverse students
- Include the acknowledgement of ethnic and cultural diversity within the curriculum and its instructional delivery.

Coupled with Stephen Benham's idea of being culturally responsive, that is to "welcome students without reservation through open dialogue, clear communication, and self-reflection" (2003), the class I sought to provide my students will not only equip them with specific skills and knowledge, provide a safe environment for every individual voice to be heard, but empower them with a sense of community as a way of thinking.

Therefore, upon setting up this module, I profiled the students' ethnic and cultural backgrounds and their experience with music. I studied their music performance proficiency and academic pathways to determine the types of music and modes of performances they can accomplish, might enjoy, or would accept. I investigated their access to technology and equipment. Lastly, I looked at ways to facilitate open dialogue, critical reflection, and to build a sense of community. Piecing together these four lots of information, I evaluated the opportunities for successful and meaningful transmissions of knowledge, through the lens of Lasalle's culture and values, which is to "promote the significance of the arts to effect personal, social, and economic transformations..." through the "development of high-level skills, creativity and critical reflection" (Lasalle, 2021).

PHILOSOPHY STATEMENT

Praxialism champions the notion of what music is good for (Regelski, 2005), and values the voices of students and their diverse yet unique experiences, embracing all types and hierarchies of music, including pop music, commonly thought of as a subordinate, too "standardized", and not a serious enough type of music (Adorno, 2000). Believing that artistic knowledge is created by constant interaction and contention with the norms, I designed this curriculum with the intention of enabling my students to create their own situated and contextually responsive knowledge by:

- Providing a conducive environment for learning through respect and inclusivity
- Facilitating understanding through awareness and constant dialogue
- Creating opportunities for reflection
- Cultivating a desire for ubiquitous learning and 21st century skillsets.

MUSICAL INTERESTS OF CHINA STUDENTS

Because it was the module's first semester, I used Lasalle's student profiles as a gauge for the China students. Lasalle offers music diplomas and degrees in several pathways: Western classical performance, jazz performance, and pop performance, composition, and electronic music. They typically enjoy Western pop, Korean pop, Mandopop, and independent (local) music. Western pop here refers to the US Billboard Top 40s and UK Top 40s, covering hip hop and electronic music, with artists like Justin Bieber, Dua Lipa, and Kanye West. Korean pop refers to the genre of music originating from South Korea. Some of these Korean pop stars also have huge followings in the US and UK, such as, BTS, SuperM, Big Bang, Girls' Generation, and Black Pink. The torchbearers of Mandopop of recent years are no longer the Taiwanese, but Singaporeans and Chinese from mainland China, with some of its biggest stars being Singapore's JJ Lin and China's Hu Yan Bin, and a new generation of China's Dou Yin–China's Tik Tok–artists. Independent music, otherwise, affectionately known as "Indie" music, is original music from Singapore, helmed by an increasing pool of singer-songwriters not contracted to a record label.

IMPLICATIONS OF TEACHING MUSIC IN A VIRTUAL CLASSROOM

The internet as a pre-requisite

Unlike the physical classroom, where the student needs to be physically present, the virtual classroom requires the provision of an internet connection. With good internet connection, the student can enjoy the full lesson as it was intended, but with poor internet connection the student can encounter a lag, where video is not synchronised with sound, causing disruption in the receiving and sending of information, affecting participation and classroom activities, and resulting in a poor learning experience. As recent as 2020, issues with the internet affecting online classes still prevailed (The Irish Times, 2020). To resolve this, I had to provide digital resources, such as, readings, weblinks, and YouTube videos to allow my students to do their own self-study before and after lessons and focus on in-class discussions understanding. I also recorded the lessons for my students to revise.

Things we take for granted in a physical classroom

The first thing we take for granted is sound as a natural phenomenon. In a physical classroom, the teacher walks into the class and starts the lesson by either taking attendance or simply talking. Because virtual classrooms require the interface of a computer and software, sound - and sometimes picture - is not as automatic as in the physical classroom. Sound and picture can be turned on and off, and their settings can pose a genuine difficulty to those with little technical and digital knowledge. A Singapore university mathematics professor realised that he did not "unmute" himself in the meeting software only after two hours into the lecture, and had to repeat the lecture (Steinbuch, 2021). To counter this, I intentionally planned a "soundcheck" before class to ensure that my students could hear me when I started each class by sharing a PowerPoint deck that has as its first slide loop a piece of music. As my student enters the virtual classroom, I prompt them via text to check their speakers. I found that I can help them resolve any technical issue before the classes and avoid affecting contact time, but this means I have to be in class earlier.

The second thing taken for granted is the range of our visibility. In a physical music classroom, I have full view of my students. I have no difficulty in shifting my gaze to observe any student practice. In a virtual classroom, however, the default view I had was the upper half of my students' bodies. As a result, much time was spent on getting my students to adjust their camera angles so I could effectively guide them on their posture, intonation, and practice. To lessen the impact of this inconvenience, I prepared video tutorials on how to set up personal cameras and manage the sound settings for virtual classes. As a result, it took longer to prepare and deliver the same amount of content online as compared to the physical classroom (Skordis, Haghparast, Batura, Hughes, 2015).

INTERACTION, LEARNER PARTICIPATION, AND SENSE OF COMMUNITY

Learning is a social process (Johnson, 2008), and interaction is the "single most important activity in a well-designed distance education experience" (McIssac, Blocher, Mahes & Brasidas, 1999). With the virtual classroom, students learn remotely and often without their peers. This removes the interaction between classmates and causes a sense of learner isolation, muting the overall learning experience (Skordis, Haghparast & Hughes, 2015). In the virtual classroom, where students do not naturally have the freedom to interact with their peers in the way they can in a physical classroom, the responsibility of creating a connection amongst students and building a sense of community within the class lies on the shoulders of the teacher (Huss, Sela & Eastep, 2015). To overcome this, I employed a palette of digital tools for my class activities, such as, Padlet, a cloud-based software that hosts real-time collaboration in order to share ideas; Kahoot, a game-based online learning platform for real-time quizzes; and the "breakout rooms" within Zoom, a cloud-based teleconferencing software to create interaction amongst my learners. I used these tools not just because they are online aids for teaching, but because they are my learners' preferred mode of learning (Nicholas, 2020).

THE ROLE OF THE TEACHER AND STUDENTS IN A VIRTUAL LEARNING ENVIRONMENT

If education is to inform, transform, and empower - core ideas from Paulo Freire's Pedagogy of the Oppressed (1970) - it cannot cease to renew itself. As educators, by holding on to "what worked", we wilfully disconnect ourselves from the ever-changing world around us and our students. In music education, our obsession with "methods and materials", as postulated by Thomas Regelski (2005), has blind spots that have become glaring in today's internet age. It assumes the learning disposition of all students, disregards their musical experiences and interests, and fails to consider the amount of information they can access - contributing to the marginalising of music learnt in the school context.

Frank Abrahams' (2005) example of how a middle school teacher in New Jersey found the basal music series to be useless in teaching music to the students because they were influenced by hip hop is not only a perfect example of the disconnect between what the music students love and that which the music teachers want them to learn, but it is also an indication of the lack of critical consideration of curriculum theory - that which Regelski (2005) calls "methodolatry". My students were tasked to hold up to four online performances, each about 20-45 minutes in duration, through the semester. They were encouraged to perform songs that they liked or that were meaningful to them. Therefore, they were the ones who decided on the repertoire, style of performance, and instrumentation. My role was not to *teach them what is good music*, but to *help them show me* what they regard as good music.

Technology-mediated learning grants the student and the teacher significant access to information. It is easy for students to surpass their teachers in any topic in a matter of "clicks". So, we must acknowledge that we as teachers are no longer what Alison King (1993) calls, "sages on the stage", imparting knowledge to students - assuming students to be "empty vessels" - but "guides on the side", facilitating understanding and assisting students in making their own situated connections. For my class, I employed mainly Constructivist concepts (Price, 2019), especially Vygotsky's Zone of Proximal Development (Price, 2019), where I helped my students achieve the learning outcomes through scaffolding and a series of tasks intended to sharpen their technical skills and improve the aesthetics of their performance.

STANDARDS AND ASSESSMENT

Even at the end of the module, I regarded my students as "work in progress" rather than "tried and tested", and this made assessing and evaluating less straightforward. For one, it is hard to place standardised testing. Let me provide an example. One student who was less proficient in playing an instrument chose to sing to a backing track, while another student who majored in Western classical violin performance chose to put up a pop trio performance. The student who performed with the backing track spent time removing the vocals from the backing track with an audio software, while the classically trained student put in hours rehearsing with the other musicians of the trio. It would be unfair if I had assessed them on the complexity of music performed. Rubrics had to be adjusted to be more accommodating, in a way that celebrates musical diversity and proficiencies without sacrificing learning outcomes.

CONCLUSION

Virtual Live Music Performance and its likes will lead a new wave of online music education for online music, where both teachers and students not only embrace ethnic and cultural diversity, but also infuse their music performances with up-to-date and emerging digital technologies, all, as such, testament to the fast-changing ways of all things online. It is paramount that educators embrace and learn to negotiate new areas and ways in which their practice can perpetuate in an increasingly virtual education landscape.

Shawn Kok is a Senior Lecturer and Member of the Academic & Examination Board at Hitmaker Global Academy; Lecturer at Lasalle College of the Arts and the National Institute of Education Singapore.

REFERENCES

Abrahams, F. (2005). The application of critical pedagogy to music teaching and learning. Visions of Research in Music Education, 6.

Adorno, T.W. (2000, January). On popular music. Soundscapes. *https://www.icce.rug.nl/~soundscapes/DATABASES/SWA/On_popular_music_1.shtml*

Benham, S. (2003). Being the other adapting to life in a culturally diverse classroom. Journal of Music Teacher Education, 13(1), 21-32

Freire, P. (1970). Pedagogy of the oppressed. New York, NY: Continuum.

Gay, G. (2000). Culturally responsive teaching: Theory, research, and practice. New York: Teachers College Press

Gay, G. (2002). Preparing for Culturally Responsive Teaching. Journal of Teacher Education, 53(2), 106-16

Hein, G.E. (1991). Constructivist learning theory. Exploratorium. *https://www.exploratorium.edu/education/ifi/constructivist-learning*

Huss, J. A., Sela, O., & Eastep, S. (2015). A case study of online instructors and their quest for greater interactivity in their courses: Overcoming the distance in distance education. Australian Journal of Teacher Education, 40(4): 72-86 *http://dx.doi.org/10.14221/ajte.2015v40n4.5*

Johnson, V.M. (2008). Learning as a social process. Veronica Johnson.

King, A. (1993). From sage on the stage to guide on the side. College Teaching, 41(1), 30-35. Kruse, A. J. (2016). 'They wasn't makin' my kinda music': A hip-hop musician's perspective on school, schooling, and school music. Music Education Research, 18(3), 240-253. *https://doi.org/10.1080/14613808.2015.1060954*

Lasalle College of the Arts. (2021, May 15). In Wikipedia. *https://en.wikipedia.org/wiki/LASALLE_College_of_the_Arts*

McIssac, M. S., Blocher, J. M., Mahes, V., & Vrasidas, C. (1999). Student and teacher perception of interaction in online computer-mediated communication. Educational Media International, 36,121-131

Nicholas, A.J. (2020). Preferred learning methods of generation Z. Salve Regina University. *https://digitalcommons.salve.edu/cgi/viewcontent.cgi?article=1075&context =fac_staff_pub*

Price, D. (2019). Constructivism as a theory for teaching and learning. Simply psychology. *https://www.simplypsychology.org/Zone-of-Proximal-Development.html*

Price, D. (2019). The zone of proximal development and scaffolding. Simply psychology. *https://www.simplypsychology.org/constructivism.html*

Regelski, T.A. (2002). On "methodolatry" and music teaching as "critical" and reflective praxis. In Philosophy of Music Education Review, 10(2): 102-104.

Regelski, T. A. (2005). Curriculum: Implication of aesthetic versus praxial philosophies. In D.J. Elliott (Ed.) Praxial music education: Reflections and dialogues. (pp. 219-248). Oxford University Press. *https://doi.org/10.1093/acprof:oso/9780195385076.003.12*

Skordis, W., Haghparast, H., Batura, N., Hughes, J. (2015). Learning online: A case study exploring student perceptions and experience of a course in economic evaluation. International Journal of Teaching and Learning in Higher Education, 27(3): 413-422.

Steinbuch, Y. (2021, February 10). Professor realizes end of 2-hours Zoom lecture that he was on mute. New York Post. *https://nypost.com/2021/02/10/professor-in-singapore-on-mute-for-entire-two-hour-lecture/*

Taylor, A. (2021, February 8). How Covid is 'creating' a new genre for live music. BBC. *https://www.bbc.com/news/entertainment-arts-55947209*

The Irish Times. (2020, April 3). 'Lagging wifi, internet freezes, distractions': Students on the reality of online classes. The Irish Times. *https://www.irishtimes.com/news/education/lagging-wifi-internet-freezes-distractions-students-on-the-reality-of-online-classes-1.4220198*

Chapter

5

Board meetings will never be the same

Anurag Kanwar

INTRODUCTION

COVID-19 has been a massive disrupter, globally, for all sectors[1]. While much has been written about the changes to education, working and the student experience, little consideration has been given to the role of the board of directors during a pandemic. This paper will consider the big changes as a result of COVID-19 in relation to corporate governance. For the purposes of clarity, it will focus on the New South Wales (**NSW**) experience.

CHANGES TO BOARD MEETINGS

Prior to COVID-19, the board of directors (**board**) meetings were usually held face-to-face. Companies (both listed and unlisted) were permitted to have 'flying minutes' or communicate electronically with directors only if their constitutions allowed this to occur. It is also worth noting that constitutions are not easy to amend. A company, though, can change or amend its constitution by passing a special resolution.

---

[1] *https://www.ubss.edu.au/article/the-impact-of-a-pandemic-on-the-approach-to-management-and-change/* accessed 4 January 2022

For a special resolution, at least 28 days' notice is required (for publicly listed companies) and 21 days' notice for other company types. The resolution must be passed with at least 75% of the votes in favour of the change[2].

In March 2020[3] and then in July 2021[4] New South Wales imposed strict movement restrictions (using the public health orders), the result of which made face-to-face meetings extremely difficult. NSW residents were not permitted to travel outside their Local Government Area, except in limited circumstances. Indeed, the pandemic put pressure on the notion of a traditional face-to-face meeting, and the question of how a company was to conduct its board meetings challenged companies within NSW.

In August 2021, the *Treasury Laws Amendment (2021 Measures No 1) Act 2021 (Cth)* was passed. This allowed an amendment to the *Corporations Act 2001 (Cth)*. This allowed all companies to sign documents electronically and conduct virtual company meetings. The amendment also permitted companies to send meeting documents via electronic means[5]. It is important to note this was temporary and only applicable until **March 2022**.

Presumably, the view of the government was such that COVID-19 would be over and there would be a return to face-to-face meetings[6]. It is also worth noting that given the time it took for the changes to be made to the *Corporations Act 2001*, prudent companies would have amended their constitutions to allow virtual meetings and the like.

---

[2] *https://asic.gov.au/for-business/registering-a-company/steps-to-register-a-company/constitution-and-replaceable-rules/* accessed 30 December 2021

[3] *https://www.ubss.edu.au/articles/2021/may/online-teaching-a-tale-of-two-institutions/* accessed 30 December 2021

[4] *https://en.wikipedia.org/wiki/COVID-19_pandemic_in_New_South_Wales* accessed 30 December 2021

[5] *https://asic.gov.au/regulatory-resources/corporate-governance/shareholder-engagement/faqs-virtual-meetings-for-companies-and-registered-schemes-held-on-or-before-31-march-2022/* accessed 30 December 2021

[6] *https://www.legislation.gov.au/Details/C2021B00011/Explanatory%20Memorandum/Text/* accessed 30 December 2021

PECULIARITIES OF VIRTUAL MEETINGS

Notice of Meetings

For a meeting to be held using technology, the notice of the meeting must include sufficient information to allow board members to attend the meeting using technology. The company needs to ensure that the virtual meeting is held in a way that allows all members to participate and attend[7].

Recording Attendance

In traditional (pre-COVID-19) meetings, attendance at meetings was recorded via signatures. So, how does this translate into the virtual world? Attendance at meetings is an extremely important part of corporate governance[8]. Anecdotal evidence reveals that a number of boards simply did not meet during this time. One company, on the other hand, took the step of installing TEAMS on all board members' phones. Attendance was then recorded via a photograph, and this was included in the official minutes.

While this approach should be commended, it requires investment in the form of IT infrastructure and support to the board members. Noting that some board members may not be comfortable with technology, the question then arises as to who is responsible for training board members to be technology literate. Is this the responsibility of the board member or the organisation? At the date of writing, there has been no case law on this matter, so for now this question is unresolved.

Voting and Conducting a Poll

One of the core activities of a board meeting is voting - whether that is voting for resolutions or voting on important core business. In a face-to-face meeting, usually, voting occurs with a show of

---

[7] *https://www.ashurst.com/en/news-and-insights/legal-updates/virtual-shareholder-meetings* accessed 4 January 2022

[8] *https://aicd.companydirectors.com.au/-/media/cd2/resources/director-resources/director-tools/2019/board/07236-4-13-board-minutes-fa.ashx#:~:text=There%20are%20no%20requirements%20under,requisitioned%20in%20a%20court%20action* accessed 30 December 2021

hands[9]. In a virtual meeting, chairs will need to be creative on how to record voting.

Digital Recordings of Meetings

In virtual meetings, it is often a given that the meetings will be recorded. For example, TEAMS notifies participants that the meeting is being recorded and that consent should be acquired. It often falls to the company secretary to contact the board members prior to the board meeting to obtain consent for any recordings. Digital recordings aid the minute taker in the writing up of the minutes.

There are some risks for the company. For example, digital recordings may also leave the board and company open to reputational damage, should the recordings be leaked. The company also needs to consider how the recordings are stored. It may be prudent to invest in some secure data storage facility for recordings of board meetings. In addition, the Company Risk Register will need to be updated to include the 'unauthorised access' of minutes as a risk.

Signing of Board Minutes

Section 251A of the *Corporations Act 2001 (Cth)* requires the minutes of all proceedings and resolutions of all board meetings be signed within a reasonable time after the meeting by the chair of that meeting or of a succeeding meeting. The board minutes must be approved by directors as a true record of the meeting. In a face-to-face meeting, this usually means that minutes are signed by the chair at the subsequent meeting. In a virtual meeting, one must consider how and when this is to occur. Some companies have had to use digital signature software such as DocuSign. Others have used email, regarded as sufficient in terms of signing minutes.

---

[9] *https://aicd.companydirectors.com.au/resources/covid-19/virtual-member-meetings* accessed 4 January 2022

WHS Considerations

Under the *NSW Work Health and Safety Act 2011*[10] *(No 10)*, a person is defined as a 'worker' if he/she carries out work in any capacity for a person conducting business or undertaking/ including work as (a) an employee or (b) a contractor or subcontractor.

Traditionally, this means that the company is responsible for any injuries suffered by the worker (or board member) while on site. But if a board is meeting virtually, is the company liable for injuries which occur at home? To date there has been little case law on this matter, however, the advice from the NSW Government is that employers have an obligation to maintain a safe working environment (on site or off site)[11]. A company may need to look at providing the necessary advice - in house or externally - to advise board members on workplace hazards. In addition, the company risk register will need to be amended to include this risk of board members injuring themselves at home.

CONCLUSION

The current pandemic has challenged the ways and processes of the traditional board of directors. While technology has enabled boards to meet, it has also raised some new issues that boards and the relevant organisations need to consider.

Anurag Kanwar is currently the Compliance and Continuous Improvement Director at Group Colleges Australia

---

[10] *https://legislation.nsw.gov.au/view/html/inforce/current/act-2011-010#sec.7* accessed 4 January 2022

[11] *https://www.nsw.gov.au/covid-19/business/covid-safe-business/working-from-home#:~:text=The%20Work%20Health%20and%20Safety,when%20they%20work%20at%20home.* Accessed 4 January 2022

REFERENCES

AICD *https://aicd.companydirectors.com.au/-/media/cd2/resources/director-resources/director-tools/2019/board/07236-4-13-board-minutes-fa.ashx#:~:text=There%20are%20no%20requirements%20under,requisitioned%20in%20a%20court%20action*

ASIC *https://asic.gov.au/for-business/registering-a-company/steps-to-register-a-company/constitution-and-replaceable-rules/*

ASIC *https://asic.gov.au/regulatory-resources/corporate-governance/shareholder-engagement/faqs-virtual-meetings-for-companies-and-registered-schemes-held-on-or-before-31-march-2022/* accessed 30 December 2021

Kanwar, Anurag *https://www.ubss.edu.au/articles/2021/may/online-teaching-a-tale-of-two-institutions/* accessed 30 December 2021

Lumsden, Andrew *https://aicd.companydirectors.com.au/resources/covid-19/virtual-member-meetings* accessed 4 January 2022

Whateley, Greg *https://www.ubss.edu.au/article/the-impact-of-a-pandemic-on-the-approach-to-management-and-change/* accessed 4 January 2022

Chapter

6

Things More Things Change

Tom O'Connor

HISTORY NEVER REPEATS ...?

There is nothing like two years in a pandemic to bring out all the cliches. This is not a criticism but an acknowledgment that the seemingly endless days of listening to COVID numbers, isolating at home, and trying to keep up with regulation changes has left everyone lost for words and resorting to formulaic phrases, if for nothing else than to reassure ourselves that 'this too shall pass'. Nevertheless, despite the total immersion in binge watching Netflix series or cleaning out long ignored shelves, which was the experience of many, much of society continued to function. The basic necessities of food, power and health continued, as did other activities considered vital.

While we live in a highly connected, highly technological world, there are some interesting parallels in our human history. Egan (2020) gives a vivid description of the impact of the bubonic plague, the "Black Death", in mid-14th century England. He notes that almost immediately after the outbreak, "students vacated centres of education, such as the new universities that had popped up in northern Italy, Paris and Oxford". Surprisingly, however, demand for higher education grew. Four new colleges at Cambridge were established during what might be considered the peak of the bubonic pandemic – Pembroke (1347), Gonville and Caius (1348), Trinity Hall (1350), and Corpus Christi (1352).

Enrolments at Oxford had increased by 1375, to the extent that the university had to establish New College in 1379.

In wiping out 30% of the population, that pandemic caused significant social disruption. It broke the feudal system in Europe. The shackles of a tightly bound class system began to fall away as acute labour shortages meant field labourers could shop around for the best wages. (A digressive parallel - try getting a 'tradie' in Melbourne these days!) The increased mobility and improved income of the peasantry, especially in England and Italy, meant that families who would previously have never imagined a university-bound son were now able to place their child in the path of learning (Courtenay, "Effect," 713). There was no overnight upheaval, but enough people began to see the possibility of a new path forward. The changes began with the expansion of the local feeder or prep schools, where children learned basic writing, English and Latin grammar, as well as hymns and songs to support the weekly Mass. Boys as young as 13 could expect to sit entrance exams for the universities. Such schools would eventually educate a young Willie Shakespeare and give rise to generations of poets and writers.

IMMEDIATE SIMILARITIES

There are some immediate similarities. The campuses of the major universities have certainly been relatively deserted over the last two years. Rather than build new physical campuses, however, higher education institutions have had to construct virtual campuses, and while online learning had been a feature of aspects of higher education courses, it has become the pre-eminent means of delivery in every course. As West (2022) notes, "COVID-19 has accelerated the widespread use and acceptance of online higher education delivery. From March 2020, all higher education was online delivery due to the COVID lockdowns." I hasten to add, COVID-19 will be seen as the moment when the virtual class became mainstream.

There are examples of ongoing demand, and indeed growth, in the international sector. I have been involved in the offshore delivery of VCE to China, but during the last two years, study tours, where students come to the Victorian partner school and experience

"Australian life", and, indeed, which have been a key selling point of the program, were unable to take place. Nonetheless, the foreign enrolments have generally held up. This is despite the low point of the political relationship between Australia and China and the tightening of the Chinese economy. Two schools were forced to close as they had been built as part of Evergrande housing developments which have experienced extreme financial difficulty. Of note here, is the fact that at least one school achieved top VCE results - results that elite schools in Melbourne may envy. The primary sector is also a strong market. The Beijing Foreign Language School introduced an Australian primary program into its curriculum in 2019. Indeed, it has proved to be extremely popular, expanding in each of the COVID years to the point where pre-booked enrolments will mean a doubling of classes at all levels.

While the circumstances between the 14th century and our present times certainly have differences, there is also a resonance in the response across the centuries. If the COVID experience has done anything, it has forced a prioritization of values and a concentration of the mind on what is important. Australia had a huge international education cohort which drew students largely from developing economies, from countries with low GDPs and varying opportunities. These students, most with financial assistance from their families, came with the aim of improving their futures through study. Generalizations can be dangerous, but in international terms, the limited opportunities for these students might be considered roughly analogous to the limitations experienced by the peasantry in feudal times. The social changes initiated by the plague allowed many to conceptualize a future through education, and international study today has done the same. COVID has reinforced the importance of education – and the desire - in modern society.

OXFORD 1379 - UBSS 2021

I have already suggested that this Covid era will be seen as the moment that the virtual campus came into its own. Just as New College, Oxford was a response to a changing society affected by a health emergency, so the new/virtual campus developed by UBSS is a response accelerated by our situation.

I have written elsewhere (O'Connor, 2021) about how online strategies and processes were used to support international students in offshore programs. The foregrounding of the electronic learning environment has forced changes in method, performance, and expectation. First, the method has changed for both teacher and student. The mediating devices now include the smart phone, along with the tablet, laptop and desktop computer replacing the physical face-to-face classroom, and future developments will no doubt include hybrid devices as well. So, the virtual campus is a multi-functional, multi-dimensional, multi-purpose environment and teachers need to adapt their teaching styles, their classroom performance, to this. All the resources that a teacher brings to a classroom need to be re-purposed and focused for use through these devices and, increasingly, the smart phone. Giving a class will need to be more than just a "talking head" teacher. A further challenge for teachers is the screen competition. The material that students access is highly sophisticated, well produced, and interactive, so students will have expectations about the quality of the interaction and the manner in which they engage with the teacher and the curriculum. Students, as digital natives, are living in this environment, already conducting their social lives online.

THE MEDIUM IS THE MESSAGE

Sixty years ago, Marshall McLuhan said "the medium is the message", but today "the medium is the reality". The virtual campus is built around devices and software that create an environment, and educators have to work with that environment. Moreover, this is not a passive and purely receptive environment; increasingly, our students live in a world where they contribute to and create content. This represents a challenge for the "new" campus. The methodology of virtual teaching, to remain relevant and therefore competitive, must include a recognition of all the possibilities the e-landscape offers and incorporate these into its pedagogy.

While the challenges in the development of the virtual campus today seem very distant from a medieval society ravaged by a plague, there are echoes from that time that offer some signs of hope. Egan (2020) concludes that the disruptions caused by the plague "cleared the ground for new people and new ideas to emerge". He asserts that an educational renaissance followed the plague which in time led to the historical Renaissance. We can only hope that we will experience a digital renaissance once we put COVID behind us. So, things will change, but the fact of that change is what makes our time the same as our history.

CODA

It would be remiss of me not to highlight one of the ironies in comparing the plague to our pandemic. The Black Death was spread by rats which swarmed all over medieval Europe - we can only hope that it will be a swarm of RATs which will allow us to move forward.

Adjunct Professor Tom O'Connor is currently a Secondary/Higher Education Consultant, a Member of the UBSS Academic Senate and Fellow of the UBSS Centre for Scholarship and Research

REFERENCES

Courtenay, W. 1980. "The Effect of the Black Death on English Higher Education." Speculum 55: 696-714. *http://www.jstor.org/stable/2847661*

Egan, P. 2020 The Black Death and an Educational Renaissance, *https://educationalrenaissance.com/2020/04/03/the-black-death-and-an-educational-renaissance/*

McLuhan, M 1964. Understanding Media: The Extensions of Man, Signet Books, New York.

O'Connor, T. 2021. VCE in China: a case study, in "Exploring a New Era: Hybrid, Blended and Online Learning" (ed.) Whateley, G., West, A. and Chanda A. UBSS publication. *https://www.ubss.edu.au/ubss-reports/?tab=Reports%202016%20-2022*

Chapter

7

Using continuing professional development to get ahead of the game – or at least keep up with

Greg Whateley, Dimitri Kopanakis

INTRODUCTION

The pandemic has created interesting opportunities and developments in its wash. In order to stay ahead of the game - so to speak - Continuing Professional Development (**CPD**) can be used effectively and efficiently to make certain industries and workers within those industries are kept up to date and current. One such cohort is pharmacists.

Professional development is a fundamental need in all industries and businesses. Certified and/or accredited groupings such as accountants, lawyers, teachers, nurses, doctors and engineers are all required to not only undertake professional development, it also needs to be continuous (CPD) to ensure currency and quality. Some of these professions actually stipulate the number of hours/points required annually to maintain registration and membership.

Professionals Australia provides a clear definition as a starting point - 'Continuing professional development, commonly abbreviated to 'CPD', refers to the work-related learning and development that should continue throughout your career. Professionals in some fields must complete mandatory CPD requirements in order to maintain their registration. For others it is entirely discretionary but no less important. CPD is one of the key mechanisms by which high standards of professional practice and the relevance and currency of qualifications and experience are maintained.'

Crawford (2016) highlighted the fact that many organisations/executives demonstrate a certain reluctance to endorse (and of course pay for) professional development - especially when there is no formal requirement. But he argues that CPD (no matter the industry) is essential in that it 'helps employees continue to not only be competent in their profession, but also excel in it. It should be an ongoing process that continues throughout an individual's career and that actively pursuing professional development ensures that knowledge and skills stay relevant and up to date. It also allows employees to be more aware of changing trends and directions in an industry.' Difficult to argue with when it is spelt out so loudly and clearly.

Micallef and Kayyali (2019) zero in on CPD for pharmacists specifically - 'Continuing Professional Development (CPD) has been mentioned in pharmacy since the early 2000s, both in the United States and Great Britain. CPD is required to ensure practitioners are up to date with current drugs and guidelines, and to ensure they are providing optimal patient care. CPD is self-directed, and supports the maintenance of knowledge, skills, and behaviours required for effective personal practice. With increasing new roles for pharmacists and other healthcare professionals, pharmacists need to be trained to ensure service provision and competence, wherever they work. This knowledge needs to be updated regularly to keep up to date with the changing role, with better critical thinking and collaboration. When completing CPD, it is important for the healthcare professional to recognize not just the "how", but also the "why".' This can surely be said of the Australian situation - same needs, same context.

Antley (2020) more recently argues, 'The professional world is becoming increasingly competitive and is constantly changing, so professional development and continual learning is more important than ever in being successful and achieving career goals.' This is so true across the board - and is fundamental to the pharmacy industry, specifically.

Pharmacists are essential workers and make an extraordinary contribution to the quality of life for so many people for so many reasons. To this end, continual professional development becomes an absolutely essential element of the pharmacy industry, and every effort (and resource) should be actioned to make this possible. With this understanding and commitment in mind, there are a number of issues that need close consideration. Being current and expert are essential. Remaining foremost in the minds of patients and customers as highly professional and informed professionals will directly relate to the future and the future of the business of pharmacy.

BENEFITS OF CPD

The benefits of Continuing Professional Development are numerous and in so many ways self-evident, nevertheless, a walk through the benefits is timely. A number of sources outline the benefits of CPD, and all can be extrapolated and placed in the context of the pharmacy industry and its practitioners.

Chris (2016) proposed ten benefits of CPD, including, it sharpens knowledge; it develops skills; it makes employees feel satisfied; it keeps staff up to date; it enhances business reputation; it makes new contacts and develops networks; it bolsters retention; it re-energises ideas; it makes succession planning easier; and it offers benefits to the organisation as a whole. Evidently there are benefits for both employee and employer.

Half (2017) proposed six benefits of professional development - you increase the collective knowledge of your team; you boost employees' job satisfaction; you make your company more appealing; you attract the right kind of candidates; you aid your retention strategy; and you make succession planning easier. Again, the underlying theme is mutual benefit.

Business Advice UK (2019) stress the benefits of professional development in terms of employee gains and suggest CPD provides an employee with the opportunity to - demonstrate an ability to self-improve; keep qualifications up to date; stay on top of the latest developments; network with like-minded professionals; and up-level a CV.

Kaplan Solutions (2021) clearly articulate five key benefits of CPD, including that it increases retention; builds confidence and credibility; makes succession planning easier; re-energises staff; and improves efficiency.

There appears little doubt - irrespective of the number of benefits articulated by the various thought leaders - that CPD brings about both improvement and change and clearly makes a solid contribution to the domains of retaining staff, improving expertise, and providing succession options that would not be possible otherwise. At the heart of training and CPD is the notion of ensuring that the pharmacy profession (and the pharmacists associated) maintain the well-earned reputation as a trusted source of health information and support. Fundamental to ensuring profile and reputation is maintaining professional competence. Clinical guidelines and recommendations are changing all of the time, and therefore, remaining current and at the same time maintaining adaptability and expertise are vital. There is enormous comfort that comes with interfacing with a confident and informed professional - no matter what industry or sector.

CPD will manifest itself in improved patient care and health outcomes. Currency is vital to this aspect. Linked closely is the enhancement of the patient/client experience and subsequently improved levels of satisfaction. CPD has enormous potential to improve workflow at all levels and at the same time decrease the likelihood of clinical/administrative errors that inevitably occur - the importance of training in this domain should never be underestimated - even in the case of experienced practitioners. Looking at all things from a fresh perspective is frequently both rewarding and satisfying for practitioners.

Improving and enhancing pharmacy staff communication skills as well as contributing to job satisfaction and job outcomes are also highly enhanced through appropriate training and CPD. With the correct focus and approach, significant dividends are inevitable.

WHAT DOES CPD FOR PHARMACISTS LOOK LIKE?

Essential to developing the most effective and immediate mode and model of CPD for pharmacists will require a significant amount of contextualising and 'insider information'. Enter the *Australasian College of Pharmacy* (**ACP**) and its support Academic Advisory Board. Without question, the most logical source of 'what pharmacists need to know' is the pharmacist. Using the various expertise and harvesting tools available - knowing what pharmacists need becomes both doable and highly accurate.

Pharmacy standards are in place and maintained by the *Australian Pharmacy Council* (**APC**). Quality assurance of CPD can be (and should be) closely aligned with and guided by accreditation and standards. The role of both accreditation and the maintenance of standards essentially form the basis of CPD content and consideration. The best type of professional development is steeped in currency and immediacy, and is always mindful of changing circumstances, legislation, and practice. We have recently experienced a significant set of developments (not to mention pressures) within the pharmacy industry. The role of the pharmacist has been augmented and profiled like never before.

There are numerous modes of delivery available to ensure effective and meaningful learning. Interactivity always plays a major role. Matters of flexibility and relevance are also starring features of any effective approach - especially for busy professionals. Modes of delivery become very important considerations, and the options are considerable. Online delivery, blended delivery and hybrid delivery options can be explored, and may include webinars, podcasts, articles, face-to-face (**F2F**) workshops and you tube items.

In recent times (courtesy of COVID-19), we have seen a seismic shift in teaching methodology and style - especially at postgraduate level. Flexibility has replaced the 'one size fits all' regime, and as a result of this, professional development now is able to embrace a range of pedagogies available. Blended Learning (a mix of online and F2F) becomes an important player in the higher education sector - and will probably be the dominant mode for some time, at least on the Australian scene.

West (2021) reminds us that Blended Learning (**bLearning**) has been with us for many years - but focus has been sharpened in more recent times. He believes 'as blended learning has developed over the last 15 years, distinct models of bL have emerged. By understanding these different models, bL pedagogy and learning design is maximised.' The blended mode also provides the option of part in situ and part in classroom - this can be both effective and cost saving.

CPD for pharmacists needs to embrace these changes to mode and pedagogy and embrace the fact that we now have options at our fingertips that were not there perhaps two or three years ago. The leaps and bounds in technology, for instance, make it possible to provide a range of activities, by way of CPD, that provide convenient and relatively low-cost options. This space needs to be explored and developed.

CONCLUSION

CPD is a vital aspect of business survival. CPD provides a range of benefits for both the organisation and individual - both tangible and intangible. The pharmacy industry is no exception to this thinking - in fact, given the importance of currency and relevancy, CPD becomes an essential component, moving forward. Part of the thinking will be the use of new and emerging technologies to provide learning and instruction options.

Emeritus Professor Greg Whateley is currently the Deputy Vice Chancellor, Group Colleges Australia. He is also a member of the Academic Advisory Board of the Australasian College of Pharmacy.

Dr Dimitri Kopanakis is currently the Chief Executive Officer of the Australasian College of Pharmacy. He is also an Adjunct Professor at the Universal Business School Sydney/Melbourne.

REFERENCES

Antley (2020) *https://www.webce.com/news/2020/07/16/professional-development#:~:text=The%20purpose%20of%20professional%20development%20is%20to%20give%20professionals%20the,knowledge%20base%20for%20your%20field*

Australasian College of Pharmacy *https://www.acp.edu.au/*

Australian Pharmacy Council *https://www.pharmacycouncil.org.au/*

Business Advice UK (2019) *https://businessadvice.co.uk/business-development/the-benefits-of-professional-development/*

Chris (2016) *https://www.josephchris.com/10-benefits-of-professional-development*

Crawford (2016) *https://www.bizjournals.com/bizjournals/how-to/growth-strategies/2016/09/professional-development-matters-success-company.html#:~:text=Professional%20development%20helps%20employees%20continue,but%20also%20excel%20in%20it.&text=Actively%20pursuing%20professional%20development%20ensures,and%20directions%20in%20an%20industry*

Half (2017) *https://www.roberthalf.com/blog/management-tips/professional-development-training-a-win-for-the-entire-team*

Kaplan Solution (2021) *https://www.kaplansolutions.com/article/5-benefits-of-professional-development*

Micallef and Kayyali (2019) *https://scholar.google.com.au/scholar_url?url=https://www.mdpi.com/2226-4787/7/4/154/pdf&hl=en&sa=X&ei=KzPrYbWLKIqL6rQP9ZGweA&scisig=AAGBfm2teAcliBKTNS_aGLnbm5eM26hEMg&oi=scholarr*

Professionals Australia *http://www.professionalsaustralia.org.au/australian-government/blog/the-importance-of-continuing-professional-development/*

West (2021) *https://www.ubss.edu.au/media/2716/what-is-meant-by-blended-learning.pdf*

Using continuing professional development to get ahead of the game – or at least keep up with

Chapter

8

Will the Great Resignation accelerate the Great Outsource and the Great Automation?

Stephen JK Parker

INTRODUCTION

The term "The Great Resignation" was coined by Anthony Klotz, Associate Professor, Mays Business School, Texas A&M University (Washington Post 2021) and has been popularised in the mass media.

In broad terms, it is presented as a phenomenon that describes record numbers of people voluntarily leaving their jobs as their local economies emerge from the COVID-19 pandemic. In the USA, this "monthly Quit rate", after initially falling at the start of the pandemic, steadily grew during 2021 to over 3%, well above the long-term maximum rate of 2.4% (World Economic Forum 2021). In Australia, the delayed emergence from COVID lockdowns suggests that this trend will occur during 2022.

The extended disruption to working patterns, whether working from home or even being furloughed, has given employees a rare chance to evaluate their work circumstances. According to Koltz (Washington Post 2021), there are four primary drivers:

- A backlog of people who would have quit, but due to COVID-19 stayed put.
- Burnout, from frontline workers to the executive suite.
- Pandemic epiphanies, where people have fundamentally reassessed their goals and identity.
- A desire to remain working remotely rather than return to the office.

The Harvard Business Review identifies 30 to 45-year-old employees as those experiencing the greatest increase in resignation rates, sitting across both Gen X and Millennial age groups (Harvard Business Review 2021). A positive consequence of this is the extensive discussions about the empowerment of the employee and how employers will need to enhance their working conditions to either retain existing and/or attract new staff. A report for the Australian Tax Office by UNSW provided a literature review on the Future of Work: emerging trend and issues (UNSW 2021).

Despite this positivity, however, there could be a darker outlook for employees, and they should "Be careful what they wish for, lest it come true…" (Aesop 620 - 564 BCE).

If employers are unsuccessful in attracting the staff required to meet the needs of the business as they emerge from COVID-19, then they will have to consider alternatives. The two options in response to the requirement to replace staff, of either outsourcing or process automation, are clear. Whether or not these are preferred options, when the survival of the business is at stake, all avenues will be explored.

OUTSOURCING

Although working from home (**WFH**) is not new, COVID-19 thrust businesses into an environment where it was the norm rather than the exception. To survive, businesses and especially their managers had to adapt their management styles and processes. For example, there was a shift from a task management orientation to an outcome based one, with trust rather than detailed oversight being required (Harvard Business Review 2020). As discussed previously, overcoming these challenges through enhanced business processes et al, has created the potential for an exciting new working environment for employees.

The process changes that ensured WFH was effective, however, have also allowed businesses to ask the question:

> If the role can be carried out effectively by somebody working 50 km from the office, why not 5000 km away, by a highly skilled person at half the cost?

Outsourcing is not new, and it does not have to be offshore, but it has traditionally been focused on areas perceived to be "low value add" or with "simple, easily replicable processes", for example, call centres. The rise of China as the "World's Factory" has shown how, with the right incentives, the traditional barriers of distance, legal frameworks, etc. can be overcome.

Not all jobs can be outsourced offshore, for example, the local plumber, and even for local employment, there are limitations to the jobs that can be delivered from home. A report from the University of Chicago finds that only 37% of jobs can be performed entirely at home (Jonathan Dingel 2020). Advances in technology and the enhanced remote/WFH processes, nevertheless, has opened outsourcing to a much broader scope of business activities that would previously have been considered too complex.

Between 1997 and 2017, the rate of casual employment (one measure of outsourcing) in the Australian labour market has remained steady within a 23.7-25.7% range. But, looking further back to the 80s through to the late 90s, there was a steep rise from 13% (1982) to 24% (1997). These changes have been attributed to the combined effects of two major recessions and the weakening of unions, both of which weakened workers' "bargaining power" (Australian Broadcasting Corporation 2018).

The recovery from the COVID-19 induced global economic shock and the labour market dynamics of the Great Resignation could create the conditions for a similar growth in workforce casualisation and outsourcing, as occurred in the 1980s and 90s.

Interestingly, this is foreshadowed in "The Age of Unreason" (Handy 1989), where the concept of "The shamrock organisation … a form of organisation based around a core of essential executives and workers supported by outside contractors and part-time help" is explored.

AUTOMATION

The option to reduce the reliance on human resources by increasing automation is nothing new. Throughout human history, "technology" has been used to replace human effort, with market dynamics and supply/demand imbalances creating the necessity that is the mother of invention. For example, the desire to share knowledge and the reliance on individual scribes to produce books created the conditions for the invention of the printing press by Guttenberg in 1440, and the desire for mass personal transport, along with the inefficiencies of existing automobile manufacturing, led to Henry Ford's production lines.

As with outsourcing, these automation efforts have typically replaced well defined activities, dependent on physical human effort. Even modern computer automation has been driven by the ability to increase the speed and accuracy of repetitive human tasks. Humans were still essential for the activities requiring "intelligence", however, with an improvement in the understanding of even complex "intelligent" processes and the democratised access to advanced computing capabilities, especially the Internet of Things (**IoT**) and Artificial Intelligence (**AI**), the scope of what can be automated has been significantly extended.

Physical robots have been used in factories for many years, but enhanced capabilities are leading to the ability to carry out more sophisticated tasks that would previously have been considered to require the flexibility of humans. A growth area for this is robots in retail environments, robots carrying out variable tasks driven by human interaction. One such example is NISKA Retail Robotics, where complex robotic synchronisation delivers almost unlimited variations of scooping, topping and delivery of high end "gelato" ice-cream (Niska 2022).

Software robots (**bots**) are expanding the scope further with Robotic Process Automation (**RPA**) and Robotic Worker Automation (**RWA**) now in use. Complex processes requiring contextual, cognitive based reasoning to determine subsequent steps are now possible. One example of this is in the legal profession where RPA can carry out e-discovery and contract management at almost unlimited scale and speed (American Bar Association 2019).

In tight labour markets, there may be no staff available, and even if there is, then it is on terms that strongly favour the employee. This is naturally a positive position for employees who can get a job, but for businesses, this can leave them with no option but to look for alternatives. The increasing capability and democratised access to RPA, along with the higher costs of engaging staff, could create a perfect storm of more favourable cost/benefit investment calculations for these alternatives.

CONCLUSION

Whether it be the 19th century Luddites destroying textile machinery in the UK, dystopian futures presented in popular culture or the cry of "the robots are coming", society has demonstrated its concerns about change.

There will be practical investment, process knowledge and skills-based challenges at the business level and also potentially significant issues at the highest stakeholder level that will need to be addressed:

- Political - What are the changing needs of society?
- Financial - Where and what is considered a taxable worker?
- Skills - How do future experts learn their skills?
- Privacy/security - How is the unethical use of shared data managed?

These practical, political, and social challenges may create change barriers and mean that outsourcing and automation are not a business's first choice. Nevertheless, directors have a fiduciary duty to act in the best interests of the businesses they represent, and that will require them to consider all options, especially if the Great Resignation has put them in survival mode.

Stephen J K Parker, is an Assistant Professor at UBSS, specialising in Innovation and Entrepreneurship

REFERENCES

Aesop. 620 - 564 BCE. Aesop's Fables

American Bar Association. 2019. Robotic Automation Can Improve Your Practice. 01 07. Accessed 01 20, 2022. *https://www.americanbar.org/groups/law_practice/publications/law_practice_magazine/2019/JA2019/JA19PerySimon/*

Australian Broadcasting Corporation. 2018. Fact check: Has the rate of casualisation in the workforce remained steady for the last 20 years? 17 04. Accessed 01 20, 2020. *https://www.abc.net.au/news/2018-04-17/fact-check-casualisation/9654334*

Handy, Charles. 1989. The Age of Unreason.

Harvard Business Review. 2020. Remote Managers Are Having Trust Issues. 30 07. Accessed 01 20, 2022. *https://hbr.org/2020/07/remote-managers-are-having-trust-issues*

Harvard Business Review. 2021. Who Is Driving the Great Resignation? 15 09. Accessed 01 20, 2022. *https://hbr.org/2021/09/who-is-driving-the-great-resignation*

Jonathan Dingel, Brent Neiman. 2020. How Many Jobs Can Be Done at Home? 06 04. Accessed 01 20, 2022. *https://papers.ssrn.com/sol3/papers.cfm?abstract_id=3569412*

Niska. 2022. Niska Retail Robotics. 20 01. Accessed 01 20, 2022. *https://niska.com.au/*

UNSW. 2021. Future of Work Literature Review: Emerging trends and issues. 09. Accessed 01 20, 2022. *https://www.unsw.adfa.edu.au/sites/default/files/documents/Future_of_Work_Literature_Review.pdf*

Washington Post. 2021. Transcript: The Great Resignation with Molly M. Anderson, Anthony C. Klotz, PhD & Elaine Welteroth. 24 09. Accessed 01 20, 2022. *https://www.washingtonpost.com/washington-post-live/2021/09/24/transcript-great-resignation-with-molly-m-anderson-anthony-c-klotz-phd-elaine-welteroth/*

World Economic Forum. 2021. What is 'The Great Resignation'? 29 Nov. Accessed 01 20, 2022. *https://www.weforum.org/agenda/2021/11/what-is-the-great-resignation-and-what-can-we-learn-from-it/*

Chapter

9

If you can read this, you're too close

Lauren Whateley

INTRODUCTION

At the start of the pandemic, I knew I had to switch gears. I had been working in education and the writing was on the wall that enrolments would plummet, borders would shut and something grim was coming. I accepted a welcome (and fortunate) paid out redundancy and bunkered down.

With my newly found free time, I redirected my energy into studying again. I signed up full-time and knocked out a year of my bachelor's online in the first lockdown (2020). This mode of study was refreshing to me – less demand of my time, I could work from the comfort of my home and didn't have to commute on public transport (paranoid at the sound of every sneeze or cough). I watched lectures, tutorials, workshops, master classes all from the comfort of my swivel chair. I met teachers and peers and worked collaboratively with people in the tropics of Queensland and in the hinterland towns of Victoria. One thing we all had in common – isolation. For many of my friends and peers, the lockdown hit a pause on all progress and productivity – low morale and waning motivation. Despite the fact the whole world had changed, along with life as we knew it, I felt like I had been given the gift of time – a chance to hit pause on everything else and get a head start on uni. Had life been normal, with full-time work and all of life's demands, I would not have knocked out those 12 months of school.

A NEED FOR CHANGE

Towards the end of 2020, studying full-time with no other outlet started to wear on me. I wanted to work again and stimulate myself with something different (such that would pay me at the end of the week). I trawled through job sites, blown away by how few ads there were – the smallest volume ever recorded in fact. I stumbled across one job for project and admin support for a property styling company. It sounded creative, I could work from home, and it paid well. I applied. I heard back the next day and within a 5-minute call had landed an interview. A week later, I met the CEO for coffee and walked away with the job.

What I can tell you about the property styling industry is that real estate is the most surprising, yet constant market I've ever seen. You will be surprised, as I was, by what nooks, crannies and square footage will sell for. But it always sells. Week after week, despite a global pandemic, the property demand soared and 2020-2021 saw a 40% increase in property sales nationwide.

If you don't yet have a foot in the property market, get onto it.

A CHALLENGING CHANGE TO COVID NORMAL

2021 started in higher spirits, most of us looking forward to some relief and recovery from a year like no other. Work kept me busy, as the demand for styling was at an all-time high. As the middle of the year neared, we were on a good wicket, and I was loving every minute on the job. Then June hit. What started with one hotspot in Sydney's far east, grew to 800 cases in a matter of weeks, and by the 26th of June, we were all in lockdown. Indefinitely.

The second lockdown hit harder for me. I had started to venture out again by that point, socialise with friends and family, and had begun to make plans for the rest of the year. Having had that little bout of momentum and sigh of relief, it felt so much worse when everything came to a grinding halt again. The weeks and months that followed were some of the dreariest, mind-numbing I had ever felt. My motivation for studying had waned, my work week blurred into my weekend, and I had never been so sick of my house or my housemate. I began to think that this was what the future looked like – yo-yoing between weeks of freedom and months of lockdown for the years to come.

On the 11th of October, we were free to leave our homes – but by that point, I was too scared. Case numbers were close to 1000, and even though we could now venture out and see people, it didn't feel like the smart choice.

How could we venture back to life as normal, forever scarred by what had happened? My solution – I left when I had to, and I stayed home when I could.

I went out for groceries, to exercise, to the park with friends (at a distance) and to my favourite cafes and restaurants (masked), just so I could dress up and have someone pour me a drink for a change. I also went out when my mental health urged me to – when I was feeling claustrophobic, cabin fever-y or out of sorts.

I stayed home when I didn't feel like socialising in a large group, or when I heard an unvaccinated person was attending, and sometimes when I'd accidentally heard the case numbers of the day and felt anxious for hours after.

The constant threat of the outside world felt crippling, and while I missed everything about it, my fear and concern overcame me sometimes and I stayed inside.

As the end of the year approached, I had worked out a system with which I felt comfortable. I wore a mask everywhere, only travelled to places where I could drive myself and park, and only with other people who were as conscientious as I was about everyone's safety. Luckily this was everyone at work, and we chugged along until Christmas, getting the job done, spending time together and keeping one another safe.

In the days before Christmas, I went for a routine COVID-19 PCR test to show a negative result and travel interstate freely. I had my test the morning of the 21st and didn't get my result back until Christmas Eve. 78 hours later. I had been used to the 8-hour turnaround and didn't expect the queues of people who were hellbent on getting tested before the holidays so they could travel safely and without consequence.

When I finally landed in Melbourne, I was exhausted but looking forward to finally seeing family after months of separation.

From there, people around me began to fall like dominoes, either sick with COVID themselves or close contacts to the infected and forced into self-isolation.

For the first time in many years, it was a small Christmas, many friends and family were unable to attend, spending the holidays alone in their room or in their house with only immediate family.

To think we believed we had seen the worst of it, worrying about 800 cases and rising. I flew home to Sydney in the first week of January to 70,000 positive cases. It has felt, and still feels like a ticking clock and it's not a matter of if but when we will get it.

THE MORE THINGS CHANGE...

2022 is set to be another wild and woolly one, and it's not all that surprising that even two years into this pandemic, we're still not sure of the way out. Despite having loved my time in the property styling and real estate market, I decided to leave freelance life and venture back into salaried employment.

I started this year back in education, in a role like those of the past, but in a climate unfamiliar to me. Students and teachers are underwhelmed at the prospect of a new academic year, working through the fog of blended learning, trying to motivate and inspire a new cohort of hopeful students. Many of my colleagues have battled through the last two years and are fatigued, despondent and out of ideas. They are bruised and burned, and they're doing their best. With the advantage of a couple of years out of the rat race, I have come in with fresh eyes and I can see clearly there is a lot of rebuilding needed. The landscape is unrecognisable.

I'm hoping I can relieve some pressure, forge forward and help my colleagues start something new. But I don't blame them if they're not as energised as I am. I've started the new year triple vaxxed, still paranoid it's coming for me and I'm next. All of us are unsure as to what's around the corner.

CONCLUSION

Living with COVID-19 is the path forward, or so we're being told. Could there be several more years of this? Is this just the new normal?

I can't help but be grateful for all those handshakes, hugs and hours spent in proximity without a mask and sanitiser strapped to me. How many young people might never understand that feeling of ease? I'm grateful for every hour spent in a movie theatre, every hour spent in a classroom and every moment of embrace I've had with my loved ones and friends when it didn't occur to me what germs they might be carrying.

2022 has me thinking that it's a slow trend upward from here and that maybe we're passing through the worst of it. Life is still strange, but maybe that's just how it will be from now on.

For now, we have our freedom, but I certainly don't feel free.

Lauren Whateley is currently the Communications Manager – Macleay College and The Fashion Institute

If you can read this, you're too close

Chapter

10

How COVID has changed the way I do things

Cyril Jankoff

INTRODUCTION

An event that occurs that significantly affects individuals, groups and society is deemed to be historic, even life changing. In the 20th century, World War One, the Spanish flu, the Great Depression and World War Two are regarded as the more significant events, despite other major, even catastrophic happenings. COVID-19, it may be said, is the first disruptor of the new century, and the most significant one since World War Two. I hope it will be the last, or at least the last in my lifetime. Below I will consider how COVID-19 affected one person - me.

HOW COVID HAS AFFECTED MY WORK LIFE

The effect on my business advisory practice

On a part-time basis, I still run legal and accounting practices and also a business consulting practice. COVID-19 has not negatively affected any of these three businesses, in fact, it has benefitted them. Client interactions are now rarely face-to-face, rather, they are via Zoom, TEAMS, email, or telephone.

The effect on my Continuing Professional Development (CPD)

I am a member of the Law Institute of Victoria, the professional association for practising solicitors, and CPA Australia, the association for practising CPA accountants. Both associations require me to attend CPD. The Law Institute's requirements are very prescriptive, less so, as far as CPA Australia is concerned. Between the two professions, annually I need to attend 40 hours of CPD. COVID-19 has made attending CPD far easier. Methods of obtaining CPD include attending online discussion groups; attending webinars (as a recipient, or, in many cases, I do so as a provider); writing articles; as well as presenting local, interstate, and international courses (mostly online during COVID-19). Incidentally, since the commencement of what we may call the era of COVID-19, I have not paid any money for CPD, except for membership of my discussion group. I remember, however, in the past on many occasions having to pay between $500 and $1000 per day to attend CPD sessions. Today, there is so much CPD available free of charge, that I cannot attend everything I'd like to as I would not have time to do my work.

The effect on my teaching

I facilitate non-award courses locally, interstate and internationally to business people in the areas of management of contracts, business improvement, negotiation, and procurement space. One contract required that I travel from my Melbourne home to Perth at least five times per year. I also had contracts in India and in Asia. Certainly, there is a lot of wasted time in travelling, so, now that I have been working online in the form of Zoom / TEAMS meetings and webinars, the only travel is my one-minute odyssey from my lounge room to my study. I also lecture in the higher education sector to graduate students in technical business subjects, so again, a lot of time has been saved due to COVID-19 restrictions. We are beginning to get back to face-to-face delivery, but I dare say, it is going to feel strange when I begin to travel again.

The effect on my work as an educational administrator

I am also involved in educational administration, and whilst my movements are subject to any lockdown, I am required to go into the office. COVID-19 has not affected this work greatly, except that I rarely see students in the office, as they are taught and administered online.

HOW COVID HAS AFFECTED MY PERSONAL LIFE

For some time, Melbourne was known as the world's most liveable city, now it is known as the world's most locked-down city. We were locked down due to COVID-19 for more than 260 days during 2020 and 2021. For nearly every one of those days, I exercised by walking or jogging. At the beginning of the first lockdown in February/March 2000, I noticed how relaxed people were, and remember passing a young father walking with his children - they were so happy. Now after what seems an eternity, and after more than 260 days of lockdown, the official lockdowns have gone. We have, however, the unofficial one. This is where many are so fearful of the new highly infectious COVID Omicron strain, that they just stay home unless it is vital to go outside. People seem to have already become more introverted, and it will take some time for them to bounce back. My two children, 16 and 18, were both very much affected by the restrictions, and for each, their education was severely disrupted. I asked the 18-year-old what she saw as the difference between pre and post COVID-19. She said that she is amazed that there are now so many "fringe people", people she had never seen before.

THE TOTAL EFFECT

The large reduction in travelling time and greater office efficiency have resulted in more time for scheduled work, and thus, a marginally higher income, and more time for my family and my non-work activities.

CONCLUSION

It is strange for me to say this, but I have had a form of holiday over the last two years. As mentioned earlier, prior to the onset of the pandemic, I often travelled for consultancy and education related work. So, with the exception of travelling from my lounge room to my study, and the odd trip between lockdowns, I have been able to use this extra time for business and personal purposes.

Cyril Jankoff is an Associate Professor at UBSS, and is Programs Director of the Melbourne Campus and EDM MBA

Chapter

11

Coping with volatility in business

Daniel Bendel

INTRODUCTION

I worked for a large successful company where the CEO believed that after a few years senior management became a little complacent. Complacency is the secret business killer, as the seeds of future failure are sown despite current success. Every few years he would ask what we would do if we were an external party wishing to buy our business. He had over the years bought many businesses and felt the experience was valuable.

Things are always changing around us - the international and Australian economy, competition, the market, consumer trends, to mention just a few.

He shared a story of a company he took over in the 1960s that had a great customer base - but was losing money. They had a meticulous stocktaking system and knew to the centimetre (maybe inches in those days!) where to locate each item of stock. The problem was they had a large team of accountants to work on this. Did they need that level of precision? My CEO was more pragmatic and was happy with a reasonable error of margin.

Our stocktaking system still took a lot of manpower, with a huge effort two times per year in December and June. Over the years, stocktaking has evolved much further, so that these days, best practice is running a good computerised perpetual stock monitoring system using cycle counting to verify.

If your business is not up with the latest best practice in any business area, you will be left vulnerable when there is a squeeze.

COVID-19 is for most of us the biggest world disrupter akin to going through a war. In fact, at the time of writing, we hear daily statistics of death and I feel we have almost become battle hardened. A few years ago, I would not have believed that we would be in this position. Just like in the aftermath of a war, some people will get back to normality and many others will have been dramatically affected.

INTERVIEWS WITH BUSINESS ENTREPRENEURS ON COVID-19 CRISIS

Certainly COVID-19 is more than just the usual disruption, but in our recently published UBSS book, 'What can we learn from Everyday successful Australian entrepreneurs?' (Jankoff and Bendel, 2021), we noted that most of the fifteen entrepreneurs interviewed considered they could have been much better prepared for the COVID-19 onslaught.

In essence, COVID-19 is just another example of volatility that can affect business.

In *Question 12* of the book, we asked how COVID-19 impacted business -

- All our respondents had been dramatically affected and, in some cases, raised concerns over a real threat to future viability.
- The physical and mental stress was apparent.
- "Good staff" were seen as a key asset to help navigate the way forward.

Question 13 - What lasting impact do you think it will have on your business?

- The pandemic is a wakeup call and businesses need to be better prepared.
- More creative ways of delivering products and service and investment in technology is the key moving forward.
- Many saw that uncertainty needs to be expected in the future.
- There was general optimism that if they can just get through this, then customers will eventually be keen to come back.

Question 14 - What have you learned that you will now implement in your business? Responses included -

- Work more online, with this generally accepted as necessary.
- Hire a good PR and marketing consultant.
- Adapt to flexible styles of learning.
- Keep looking at alternative distribution channels.
- Recognise the importance of networking and the need to keep obtaining business advice.
- Accept a less than optimal result due to things being outside of your control.
- Ensure access to spare working capital and finance.
- Be vigilant on health and safety in workplaces.
- Keep up to date with government regulations.
- Ensure there is a risk management system in your business.
- Ensure the ability to make quick decisions.

All our respondents emphasised the need to relax and keep things in perspective.

WHAT CAN WE DO TO RECOVER?

Buy your business back

When a due diligence is undertaken, the business is evaluated from a SWOT analysis (Strengths, Weaknesses, Opportunities, and Threats) perspective, including plenty of checklists that range from administration through to sourcing and marketing.

What would you keep? What would you eliminate? Which employees would you keep? What parts of the business need to be streamlined? What are new opportunities that have been neglected? Do you have too many products or too few?

Pace of change

We live in a world of great change and will continue to do so. We need to keep pace or be left behind. We need to identify those aspects and how important they are.

Perseverance and resilience

Most of our entrepreneur respondents in our book emphasised the need for perseverance. I think they sometimes meant resilience. They are similar, that is, in that there is the need for an ability to face problems, but then also the need to keep going in spite of obstacles.

Not all businesses have been affected in the same way. One of these entrepreneurs was involved in the 'pet foods industry', so they were relatively safe. One of our respondents, however, was involved in the tourist industry - they had to put the business on hold and structure their business as best they could in order not to lose too much money. The importance of cash reserves again was key.

One way of categorising these businesses to transform their business model to build resilience…

BUSINESS TRANSFORMATION BOARD

Inclusiveness

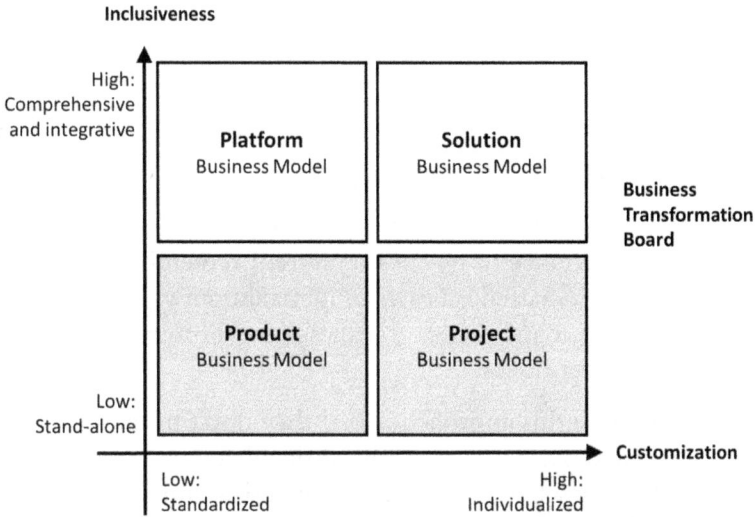

Figure 2 - Business Transformation Board
(www.weforum.org/agenda/2020/11/transform-business-model-post-covid-future/)

Within each industry, there are four types of business models as indicated above. The more the business is inclusive, the better off they will be during times of crisis - because they demonstrate more resilience.

Inclusiveness is achieved by comprehensive and integrated offerings, for example, a recurring transaction such as a subscription or an offering that wraps around the customer with premium product and an almost family feel to the business.

McKinsey puts this in another way - "Those organizations that are making the shift from closed systems and one-to-one transactional relationships to digital platforms and networks of mutually beneficial partnerships have proved more resilient during the crisis."

Growth and scalability

In the book, 'Business War Stories from the Trenches' (Jankoff and Bendel), in chapter 2 we talk about the need to work out what the size of the business needs to be - perhaps because of COVID-19, this issue may need a re-think.

Business culture and people

One key element that I picked up from our entrepreneurs is the issue of the importance of business culture. I remember one business that was focused on extracting maximum value from their staff worked their management to excessive overtime, working on weekends and after hours.

The problem with this approach is that they don't have "staff credits" stored away. In other words, if they had been more flexible in the good times, when there is a genuine crisis and they ask staff to sacrifice, then staff would be more willing to "put in".

It is important to appreciate the right talent, regardless of hierarchy.

One of our entrepreneur respondents employed a young person on an overseas holiday/working visa. During the last couple of years, she has shown herself to be a highly talented person, restructuring the production planning documentation, the quality control documentation, website design and many other related tasks. They are trying to hold on to her, but know that once she gets Australian citizenship, she is likely to take a much more highly paid job somewhere else. In the meantime, they are encouraging her to take on a variety of responsibilities and paying her what they can afford.

The future

Just when we thought we were seeing the end of the pandemic in 2021, along came the Omicron variant (using the 15th letter of the Greek alphabet). At least we are learning the Greek alphabet!

I personally feel that the government threw too much money around with few control measures and too early on. I guess government felt it did not matter, as long as money was pumped into the economy to save businesses from collapse. But such huge amounts of money thrown about has left the government without much left in the bag for the unanticipated extended COVID-19 period. All that money being pumped in suggests that inflation is likely to rise…but who knows?

Indeed, businesses should be getting ready for the next challenge.

Daniel Bendel FCPA is a Fellow of the UBSS Centre for Entrepreneurship

REFERENCES

Jankoff, C and Bendel, D (2021) "What can we learn from Everyday successful Australian entrepreneurs?" Smart Questions

Jankoff, C and Bendel, D (2020) "Business War Stories from the Trenches" Smart Questions

https://www.mckinsey.com/featured-insights/future-of-work/from-surviving-to-thriving-reimagining-the-post-covid-19-return Accessed 27/01/2022

https://www.weforum.org/agenda/2020/11/transform-business-model-post-covid-future/ Accessed 27/01/2022

Chapter

12

Waves from the Effects of COVID-19 on a Music Business

Art Phillips

INTRODUCTION

This article examines the innovation of an Australian-based company, *101 Music Pty Ltd®*, its product lines, customers, and income streams. The changes that occurred - from the effects of the COVID-19 pandemic and the hiatus of television and visual content productions around the world due to social distancing measures and isolations - have resulted in a catastrophic downturn of licensing and performance income in the music soundtrack industry.

MUSIC – PROVIDING EMOTIONAL SOLUTIONS TO STORYLINES

When we think of music, we generally recall the famous classical pieces, the popular radio hits and the theme music from television and feature films that take us on those memorable emotional journeys.

Composing music is a creative art form and can serve a variety of purposes, but one very important medium is music that accompanies the visual and its storyline - the television/film soundtrack. Have you ever sat and watched a film or television series stripped of its music soundtrack? If you have, you will quickly notice that the program does not have the same impact without music, as music propels stories, like an invisible character, like a third dimension. Music in a visual program moves and sways the viewer in ways that are consciously - and many times, subconsciously - designed to help underpin, guide, and define the story.

Music can either be written specifically to the visual by a music composer, or music can be licensed from existing commercial song recordings, or with the licensing of 'production library music' - the business of *101 Music Pty Ltd®*.

PRODUCTION (LIBRARY) MUSIC AND LICENSING FOR TELEVISION, FILM AND ADVERTISING CONTENT

101 Music Pty Ltd® is a production library music catalogue and record label. Production Music is music that is created, composed, produced, and recorded before we even know where it will be used. This source of music has been in existence for over one hundred years and is manufactured specifically for the synchronization or dubbing into audio-visual programs, which can include television series, documentaries, feature films, advertising campaigns (radio or television), websites, online games, music on hold, ringtones, and many other areas.

Production Music is licensed to content producers for their visual production. It has seen a surge in use and is a popular source of music licensing, especially since reality television has become a staple for viewers over the past twenty-five years. Television shows such as 'Survivor', 'Police Rescue', '60 Minutes', 'The Today Show', 'Oprah', 'Crime Story', E-Entertainment, and the like, use production music extensively. It is fast and efficient to obtain, as it is already composed and produced, making music licensing clearances (the paperwork) quite simple.

Statistics from the Production Music Association (**PMA**), an American industry association, have placed a dollar value on the revenues generated by production music for the first time, citing it as a billion dollar a year industry. As PMA Chairman and Associated Production Music President, Adam Taylor, says: *'Production Music, which is heard in most film, television and video productions, is often hidden in plain sight'* (Dillion, 2017).

THE COMPANY & BUSINESS

101 Music Pty Ltd® exports its product across 85 global territories under some 24 separate distribution agreements. Our music distributors are our agents, or as we call them in our industry, 'music sub-publishers'. 101 Music is the originating music publisher and record label, where we sub-license product under a term of 3 years, renewable for 1-year increments to the most suitable foreign sub-publisher distributor in each region. We pick and choose carefully who will represent 101's product, as the 'export market' is our lifeline. *101's distributor list can be found using the territorial flags on this menu - https://101.audio/distributors/* (Phillips, 2021).

101 Music Pty Ltd® currently has 67 production music albums in its asset portfolio, encompassing a variety of genres - from drama, sports, comedy, positive feel-good, extreme impact trailer style, travelogue, news themes, calm landscape style, to corporate, industrial, and many more. *101's releases can be viewed and heard as marketing teasers - https://101.audio/releases/* (Phillips, 2021).

The 101 music logo and name is trademarked ® across numerous territories. We also use a short sales 'slogan' to sit with the business name and logo: *emotional solutions through music.*

Figure 3 - 101 emotional solutions through music is also incorporated into the logo design

WAVES FROM THE COVID-19 PANDEMIC

The consequences of the global pandemic have been felt by my company as with so many other businesses across the world. The situation with a production music company is a little different to most other businesses, as we don't see income returns from a music licence for some 9 ~ 18 months after the agreement is made with a content producer.

And with respect to broadcast performance income, which is another income source, we don't receive this stream of income anywhere for up to 2 ~ 2.5 years after the program is aired (broadcast) to the public.

In light of these facts, I realized early on during the COVID-19 pandemic, that is, from March 2020, that my company would need to implement an effective plan to deal with the effects of this pandemic - an income downturn - which would not begin to hit my business until around March 2021. And so it did, and I am proud and fortunate to state that **101 has survived to tell the story**.

Most businesses experienced an immediate downturn of revenue as a result of the pandemic, and many were able to achieve government support by showing a 30% decline in income. My company did not see an income drop until at least a year after the beginning of COVID, making it sound like my business was not so hard hit and that I was very lucky, but actually, I was not so fortunate in many aspects - the worst was to come with a delayed effect.

I realized that television and film productions were unable to continue filming due to health regulations in every territory requiring the social distancing measures and isolations - but nobody knew for how long. I also realized that any new music licences would halt due to the reproductions from the hiatus - no filming, no new tv shows = no music being used.

I needed to take steps urgently to plan efficiently and to pave the road ahead for my company to survive. My business would either have to stop manufacturing completely in order to save on costs, or have fewer album releases per year, to compensate for the upcoming income decline. As I saw it, both of these ideas would not have been a good solution. I had to find a way to cut manufacturing costs without affecting the quality nor quantity of new product being released.

If my company stopped the creation and manufacturing of product releases completely or simply just slowed down the number of releases per year, my company would lose its optimal search/find 'algorithms', with respect to 'search results'. This would deplete substantially on each territorial website - and therefore be an additional disaster of its own kind. That is an article in itself.

After careful thought, I decided to utilize existing asset resources, by repackaging these resources to obtain a cost savings method and formula, in order to continue with product activity and output.

My theory was: let's put these assets to use by repacking select product in an innovative manner to increase exposure, and to keep the algorithms of 101 Music alive. Once the pandemic subsides, and the clients and users of my product begin searching for music to suit their needs, 101 is still on top - never having stopped producing.

101 Music already has some 1200 music titles (song titles) in its portfolio, with product previously released and active in the marketplace. These music productions have already been created, composed, produced, recorded, mixed, and mastered, and have their own metadata that accompanies their original release.

I could therein create 'compilation' album releases, using existing material, reactivating and re-packaging 12 existing music pieces that fit nicely together into a new and specific emotional album direction. Music is all about emotions, so, then, marketing the compilation album releases under an emotional descriptive banner - drama, comedy, dance, etcetera - was the direction I took.

Since 'keywording' is a critical process for every music product release, this compilation concept would be best focused by using only 'one' keyword in the album product title, such as, Calm, Summer, Mystery, and the like.

I moved forward with this by creating a sub-label for 101 Music, called **101 Music Compilations**, where I'd release the *Best Ofs, Best Of_____*.

Rather than spending, generally, AUD 10,000 per album release on manufacturing and production costs, I could cut this back to AUD

2,000 per album release by repackaging existing music from the 101 music catalogue into a new release album compilation, such as, the **Best Of Home**[12] (a suitable title to be the first in a series of 101's compilation albums, as everyone is staying home, where the music aim would be warm, cozy, safe, relaxed content). I later released **Best Of Summer**[13], then **Best Of Calm**[14] (See footnotes to better understand the sound of the music and marketing descriptions employed for these releases.

Next in the series will be **Best of Positive** (upbeat, radio friendly, feel-good).

Historically, my company releases an album every 2 months, generally 6 albums per year. Rather than spend $ 60,000 per annum, this concept would only cost $ 12,000, or possibly less. This would also keep some of my independent contractors working, with a bit of income flow during the pandemic, and give my composers the additional outlet to have their music re-released, re-packaged for additional exposure and extra performance income.

The only manufacturing work that needs to be processed on Best Ofs albums is finding 12 appropriate tracks from my existing asset catalogue - then, it is re-packaged, with fresh artwork for a new look, under a new brand, simply recompiling the metadata from its existing release to suit its repositioned genre.

These 'Best Of' compilations are like a music 'playlist' that one would create of their favourite pieces from the 60s or 70s, so to speak. With the 'Best Ofs', I achieve a savings of 80% in direct costs (costs of goods sold), which allows for a large percentage of income downturn as a safety-net.

I am now just realizing the effects of the downturn in television production from around the globe, for example, from productions - or lack of - coming out of Los Angeles, New York, UK, Japan, Germany, South Korea, and locally. Upon analysis, I am seeing a depletion of sales revenue of some 42%.

At the start of 2021, I decided to intersperse a new original album release (normal production and costs), with every second release

---

[12] *https://101.audio/portfolio-items/best-of-home-101mc001/*
[13] *https://101.audio/portfolio-items/best-of-summer-101mc002/*
[14] *https://101.audio/portfolio-items/best-of-calm-101mc003-from-101-music/*

being a 'Best Of' compilation, therein achieving enough of a cost savings to keep the company unaffected by the wave of the pandemic crisis. This way, I am not diluting 100% of new innovation for the company and am feeding a fresh asset pool of original copyrights.

From my catalogue content analysis, from the 67 album releases to date, I could continue this trend for approximately 3 years before the *compilation* approach would become overcooked, stale and mostly impractical.

Another survival method that I have employed is focusing more on music for radio ads, as the downturn of production has not affected radio much at all, as group gathered personnel and production sets are not required for these types of productions. I've now focused more on new original album releases that are positive, upbeat, radio friendly, and corporate sounding, utilizing unique one-liner song lyrics, a lyric that is the title of the music track, such as, **Let's Do It** (from Motivations, as noted below). These lyric one-liners repeat through the audio file, with a vocalist singing the hook line, but they do not have a continued lyric storyline, just the one-liner. Examples can be referenced here:

- MOTIVATIONS 101M051[15]
- RADIO FRIENDLY 101M044[16]
- TURNING CORNERS 101M041[17]

Having the one-liner song / lyric approach allows a multitude of usages, rather than it being too specific to an exact or distinct advertising story situation, therein heightening the usage possibility. A positive one-liner title - vocalized - as a purpose driven direct message works for any product. Why limit oneself to a specific advertising use? We are going for the larger game - any product, with a long and continued capacity for usage.

Radio ads have continued through any hiatus resulting from COVID and its restrictions.

---

[15] *https://101.audio/portfolio-items/new-101-music-release-101m051-motivations/*
[16] *https://101.audio/portfolio-items/101m044-radio-friendly/*
[17] *https://101.audio/portfolio-items/101m041-turning-corners/*

CONCLUSION

The above strategies have allowed strong sustainability for the business and have been a safeguard against the waves of the COVID economic downturn. The results are working, as I have begun to see just recently - now, two years since the beginning of the pandemic.

These strategies have provided positive opportunities, such as new innovative product, a new business arm (a business tributary), a farther reach for my business assets, all of which supply a stronger 'long tail effect' - income from assets that continues to grow over time.

> 'The long tail is a statistical pattern of distribution that occurs when a larger share of occurrences occurs farther away from the centre or head of distribution. This means that a long tail distribution includes many values that are far away from the mean value. In an economic context, this signifies that more products are purchased that are different from the most mainstream products' (Anderson, 2004).

Businesses need to find ways to survive during the greatest of disasters or get swallowed-up. A business plan has always been necessary for action and being aware of 'change' in one's business plan is essential.

Aside from running my own business, I lecture part-time in Entrepreneurship Research Report at Universal Business School Sydney, teaching two classes a week. I am passionate about sharing my knowledge and experiences with students.

I teach postgraduate students how to write an effective business plan, a plan as such being the only assurance in running a business smoothly. I also talk about the importance of *change*, and how necessary it is to positively embrace situations such as the pandemic.

As I quote to my students:

'Effective entrepreneurs are exceptional learners.

We learn from everything.

We learn from our clients, our customers,

our employees, our associations, our suppliers.

We learn from other entrepreneurs.

We learn from experience, from doing,

and importantly –

we learn from making mistakes.

The core to success is how you will engage with **change**.

Hurdles are our friends...

Disappointments are never our enemy' (Phillips, 2021).

Art Phillips is the owner and director of 101 Music Pty Ltd®. His bio can be found at - https://101.audio/bio-art-phillips/

Art is also an Adjunct Professor at UBSS and Director of the UBSS Centre for Entrepreneurship.

REFERENCES

Anderson, C., 2004. *https://miloszkrasinski.com/the-long-tail-effect-theory-in-practise-explained/*

Dillon, D., 2017. NewcastleStudio. *http://www.newscaststudio.com/2017/09/20/production-music-now-billion-dollar-industry*

Phillips, A, 2021. My distributor list can be found using the territorial flags on this menu here. *https://101.audio/distributors/*

Phillips, A, 2021. 101's releases can be viewed and heard as marketing teasers at *https://101.audio/releases/*

Phillips, A, 2021. As I quote to my students: *'Effective entrepreneurs are exceptional learners'*, UBSS Entrepreneurship Research Report, lecture, May 2021

Chapter

13

COVID learnings on forgiveness and optimism

Bruce Everett

COVID-19 sucks! Like some of you, we've endured 262 days of lockdown Melbourne, taking in that there have been 275 million cases globally with 5.5 million deaths, and now we have a new strain of Omicron to worry about. I feel the mass trauma. I feel it directly and vicariously. I feel for the families who are experiencing pain and loss; the frustrated teachers and the school kids; the people in the hospitality industry or SMEs who have lost their livelihood; the exhausted frontline workers; for my wife and I who can't visit family interstate; for our elders in aged care who can't be visited. We all feel grief in some way and hold grievances associated with a sense of loss but, as Dr Fred Luskin asks in his forgiveness therapy work, will we hold onto our past grudges at the expense of our present happiness?[18]

COVID-19 sucks! It is affecting our relationships at work, including in my world of commerce and contracting with supply chain disruption; with our neighbours, locally and globally; with our political leaders; with our rights and responsibilities; our relationship with what we think is right and wrong; and with ourselves, our agency, our resilience, our confidence, our compassion. When a neighbour encroaches on my territory or threatens my life and livelihood through poor health practices, as it

---

[18] Dr Fred Luskin, Forgive for Good: A Proven Prescription for Health and Happiness

sometimes feels like in lockdown Melbourne, I don't feel like loving my neighbour at all. When I go for a walk and see people without masks, you should see what goes through my mind! Why don't they have a mask on? Why DON'T they have a mask on? Should I walk around them? Should I report them? I'm not suffering directly from COVID health impacts, at least physically, but my relationships with others are suffering.

We are living amidst the first global mass trauma event since World War 2, and likely the first of such severity in our lifetime. One way to understand trauma is a rupture in "meaning-making"[19]. As psychologist, David Trickey, says, it's when "the way you see yourself, the way you see the world, and the way you see other people are shocked and overturned by an event – and a gap arises between your "orienting systems" and that event – simple stress cascades into trauma, often-mediated through sustained and severe feelings of helplessness." Helplessness, oh yeah, I felt that during the Melbourne lockdown in the second half of 2020 and again in 2021. What makes COVID-19's trauma truly "massive"[20], though, is its impact on the entire population, including those who will never catch the virus or even know people who have.

The science of trauma suggests that we should acknowledge the event and its effect on us, work through the grief (such as in the Kubler-Ross[21] 5 stage cycle of grief) and seek to mend the rupture in "meaning-making". World War 2 holocaust survivor and respected psychiatrist, Viktor Frankl, offers guidance for anyone who suffers in his book, Man's Search for Meaning, saying, "The greatest task for any person is to find meaning in his or her life." Frankl sees three possible sources for meaning: in work (doing something significant); in love (caring for another person); and in courage during difficult times. Suffering in and of itself is meaningless. We give our suffering meaning by the way in which we respond to it. "Forces beyond your control can take away everything you possess except one thing, your freedom to choose how you will respond to the situation. You cannot control what happens to you in life, but you can always control what you will feel and do about what happens to you." We can choose to work

[19] David Trickey, a psychologist and representative of the UK Trauma Council
[20] https://www.bbc.com/future/article/20210203-after-the-covid-19-pandemic-how-will-we-heal
[21] Elisabeth Kubler-Ross, 'Death and Dying', 1969

through the emotions of denial, anger, bargaining, or depression (the first 4 stages of the Kubler-Ross cycle), to get to acceptance (and meaning, which was added as a 6th stage), or we can stay metaphorically in the 'washing machine' of the initial and seemingly endless stages of the grief cycle.

So, I'm working on the 5th stage of acceptance. It's kind of a weary acceptance, yet still hopeful, which means that I'm praying for the courage to change the things I can change, accept the things that I can't change, and the wisdom to tell the difference[22]. I'm coming out the other side and developing a personal roadmap out of COVID. It's a roadmap informed by experience, especially of lockdowns, and by hope in a different future. It's informed by a better understanding of myself, of my strengths and my weaknesses. It's also informed by a search for meaning from this time of COVID. Because, why else have we gone through this experience? Do we just accept it and move on? There must be some learning and some good to come out of this.

Kübler Ross worked with David Kessler to write the book, On Grief and Grieving, and Kessler has now introduced the critical 6th stage of finding meaning. As he says, many people look for "closure" after a loss, however, it's in finding meaning which can transform grief into a more peaceful and hopeful experience. As Frankl wrote, we can find this in work, in love and in courage in these difficult times, and, as I write this, we are going through what is known as the Great Resignation, where masses of people are having the courage to change their work to achieve more flexibility and more meaning. For me, I find myself changed through this experience. I am now less attached to an uncertain future and more attached to the present. I have found meaning in what I mean to people and what they mean to me. I have found meaning in how my life choices impact others and the world. It is with a heightened feeling of compassion and connectedness that I am taking the first steps on my personal road out of COVID.

Will we hold onto the grief and grievances associated with a sense of loss and hold onto our past grudges at the expense of our present happiness?[23] Will we forgive events and the world that

---

[22] The Serenity Prayer, written by the American theologian, Reinhold Niebuhr
[23] Roberto Assagioli, "Without forgiveness life is governed by an endless cycle of resentment and retaliation"

conspire against us, others who seek our harm or don't understand our position, and even forgive ourselves for not being perfect, strong, patient, or forgiving? We do need to find meaning in suffering, including mass trauma events like this COVID-19 health, economic and social pandemic. What has COVID-19 meant for you, for your relationships, for your understanding of the world, for your understanding of yourself?

Bruce Everett is the Regional CEO for Asia Pacific for World Commerce & Contracting (www.worldcc.com), a global member association and peak body for procurement, contracting and supply chain practitioners.

Bruce also works as a chaplain for the Brotherhood of St Laurence, is on the Anglican Diocese of Melbourne social responsibility committee and has recently joined the Huber Social - Ethical Review Board.

https://www.linkedin.com/in/bruce-everett-9a8a4251/

Chapter

14

Music on screen – reflections on livestreamed concerts

Eugene Seow

INTRODUCTION

"You need to pivot," they said. "Embrace the new normal; that's how life is going to be from now on." A familiar trope directed towards artists from governments around the globe - what is more sinister may be what is left unsaid. Perhaps they imply the following: we don't value your craft, we don't have the time or headspace to help you, and you're on your own. While that may be a slightly harsh way to interpret the struggling legislations of the world when faced with the continuing onslaught of the COVID-19 pandemic, it may not be that far off from the truth. Despite the generous reliefs granted to other entertainment industry sectors, the lack of parliamentary support for nightclubs in Britain (Mizierska & Rigg, 2021) is all but proof of the lack of support from the powers that be.

As a musician with roots in session work, COVID-19 has destroyed my former career. In particularly conservative countries with authorities who choose to err on the side of caution, practically everything else is allowed to happen before live music. I have witnessed firsthand the breakdown of former colleagues who are too deeply entrenched into the persona of a gigging musician. Most of them have known only this lifestyle and career for decades. As a result, many of those waiting for the return of music have no other income generation alternative besides low-paying odd jobs.

This fact exists in parallel to the discovery made by Mizierska and Rigg (2021) of how many night-scene professionals went through the "five stages of grief, beginning with denial, namely insisting that the situation was not serious and would not last for long" (Mizierska & Rigg, 2021, p. 77). Other musicians have pivoted away from not only performing but also music completely. Many cite money as a reason, but further conversation and commiseration reveal their loss of faith in the government. Ironically, this is the very government that should promise a more prosperous, enriching life. Simply put, the poor handling by the government, with the legislation that ensued, has caused the disillusionment of many artists with unlimited potential. This is undoubtedly an incredible pity.

Those who continue to struggle have turned to one of the only other possibilities to keep the music alive: livestreaming. Musicians converted bedrooms and living spaces into camera-friendly areas with drapes, lights, and other peripherals. Using their craft to wage war on the pandemic in the only way they knew how, songbirds crooned, guitarists shredded, and, indeed, everybody poured out their hearts and souls. Though novel and a refreshing change from the coerced silence of the evening streets, these endeavours would quickly find themselves facing unprecedented obstacles and creating a host of new issues for consideration.

THE IMPORTANCE OF RITUAL – WHY MUSIC IS IMPORTANT

Human beings are creatures who need a routine to function. We often hear that one feels better (psychologically or physically) after morning coffee or a good 7am yoga session. Even something as simple as making one's bed after waking up already sets the tone for the rest of the day. Perhaps this activity also links to the oft-used phrase to "wake up on the right side of the bed".

Vandenberg, Berghman, and Schaap (2020) reference the vital role of the genre of music associated with raves to unify people. They state that the ritual of attending a concert together "can establish and ratify membership symbols, foster standards of group morality, and be conducive of individual emotional energy or confidence"

(Vandenberg, Berghman, & Schaap, 2020, p. S143). Though their study concerns electronic music, it can be easily extrapolated that all forms of music fulfil a habit-setting function in society. The authors posit, however, that the "'liveness' of livestreamed concerts is defined in terms of time, rather than space" (Vandenberg et al., 2020, p. S144). Therefore, we must expect virtual concerts' ritualistic power to pale compared to yesteryear's raves. It is, nevertheless, no surprise to find more disorientation in an overworked population with fewer avenues to enact the habitual destressing.

PHYSICAL AND SOCIAL PRESENCE

A study conducted by Onderdijk et al. (2021) examines the implications of livestreamed concerts on how much engagement is elicited from an audience. Manipulating different factors, the authors drew salient observations and conclusions that can aid in the executing of more holistic livestreams in the future, pandemic or not.

Three concerts were conducted to investigate three different aspects of audience participation. The first had audiences able to vote for songs - essentially song requests. This experiment concerned agency. The second juxtaposed participants watching the livestream with virtual reality headsets with those viewing on a normal YouTube livestream. This one sought the implications of physical presence. The final experiment compared attendance through Zoom with watching through, once again, a normal YouTube livestream; it investigated social connectedness connotations.

Regarding agency, Onderdijk et al. (2021) found that providing the participants with an option to vote had no relation with how much agency they felt. Instead, "social connection with the artist was predicted by whether their preferred song was played, regardless of their ability to vote" (Onderdijk et al., 2021, p.15). This observation is especially noteworthy because we can extrapolate that an audience cannot be, in a sense, manipulated into feeling engagement. Instead, what they feel is organic because art is, itself, organic. This acknowledgement of how agency concerns only the individual's opinions is worth keeping in mind as we examine the results of the other two experiments.

In the second and third experiments, Onderdijk et al. (2021) found that "virtual reality promoted feelings of physical presence, while Zoom promoted feelings of social presence" (Onderdijk et al., 2021, p. 22). Indeed, virtual reality showed a significant advantage over viewing a two-dimensional video in physically connecting the audience to the performance. This edge is evident because the viewer can "move around" the room instead of being forced to be static. Likewise, Zoom proved superior in connecting people socially compared to a simple (albeit live) YouTube comments section. This is because Zoom allows the audience to see each other and communicate in real-time, augmenting the impression of being in each other's presence.

Despite these experiments identifying the positives of livestreaming, one also sees its numerous shortfalls. For example, though Zoom fosters social engagement, the audience cannot be too large, or one will see only a sea of faces on the computer monitor. Also, the superiority of physically being in a room with a live performance is glaringly apparent compared to our budding virtual reality capabilities. These data will help musicians better leverage livestreams to better society. Nevertheless, live concerts must be reinstated as soon as physically possible to minimize damage to our collective consciousness.

SOCIAL RESPONSIBILITY AND ARTISTIC ENGAGEMENT

Margolies and Strub (2021) present "musical, poetical, and organizational responses to [the] coronavirus", "[providing] opportunities for examining a rich, an expansive, and an emergent musicultural discourse" (Margolies & Strub, 2021, p. 2). They examine two things: first, how livestreamed Mexican regional music can be the catalyst for social participation and second, the composition of original verses by traditional performers making commentaries on the COVID-19 pandemic (Margolies & Strub, 2021). This article, thus, concerns the more ethereal aspects of art and how it affects the underlying fibre of civilization.

Most notably, the authors found that "at a moment when governments still struggled to effectively respond to the coronavirus outbreak, community content creators such as Vera put forth solutions to a problem while also establishing a new normative connection between social responsibility and artistic engagement" (Margolies & Strub, 2021, p. 5). Therefore, as seen from how forward-looking artists and art can be, one can already make a strong case for their continued support by official channels. In fact, "in the COVID virtual huapangos, the musicians in many ways positioned their music making as a service to a community in crisis, explicitly framing their performances as expressions of resilience in the shadow of the coronavirus" (Margolies & Strub, 2021, p. 5).

Also, the compositional aspect that benefits the world cannot be understated. To put it succinctly, the performers' "new verses encouraged strategies for community preservation, sought to soothe uncertainty and fear with familiar repertory, and entertained listeners with humor in the face of isolation and nascent death" (Margolies & Strub, 2021, p. 12). Composers' potential to allay fears is enormous and cannot be ignored. Artists are already able to influence their audience. Still, composers take it a step further because of their highly honed ability to craft music. Considering specifications such as lyric writing and form manipulation, composers have the social responsibility to conciliate the populace.

Though apparent in the Mexican regional music context, one finds that artists throughout the entire world tend to seek to heal dissent with their music. Therefore, the observations gleaned from this article can apply to musicians in general. Even cover musicians select songs as homages to a tragedy or tunes to honour a person. These proliferations of positive energy and values in the ever-connected world self-perpetuate. With global problems still rampant, there can never be enough good in the world.

TAKEAWAYS FOR THE FUTURE

Things will never be the same if we do not ensure they are. Certainly, for some things, that is not a bad thing. Many factors that impact music-making were catalysed into being by the pandemic and should be embraced. For example, e-learning has evolved to such an extent that one can find an extremely comparable education entirely online in certain aspects of music.

Moreover, concepts found through studies conducted during and because of the pandemic are valuable and cannot be discounted. For one, reinforcing artists' and composers' collective power to enact social justice is paramount. Also, valuable insights into app usage such as virtual reality and Zoom can benefit many facets of society. These include inclusivity for the differently-abled who may not physically attend an event or allowing a long-distance fan to experience a musician's concert.

And yet, live music cannot be left in the annals of history. Its essentiality is crucial to developing a healthy, productive society with well-balanced lifestyles (Mizierska & Rigg, 2021). Furthermore, the visceral sensation of connecting with a myriad of souls in the same physical and mental space has no substitute. Let us all ruminate on how music has shaped us into who we are and pledge to bring live music back post-haste.

Eugene Seow is currently Academic Manager, Hitmaker Global Academy – Singapore

REFERENCES

Margolies D. and Strub J. (2021) 'Music Community, Improvisation, and Social Technologies in COVID-Era Música Huasteca'. Frontiers in Psychology. 31 May 2021.

Mizierska E. and Rigg T. (2021) 'Challenges to British Nightclubs During and After the Covid-19 Pandemic'. Dancecult: Journal of Electronic Dance Music Culture. 14 December 2021.

Onderdijk K. et al. (2021) 'Livestream Experiments: The Role of COVID-19, Agency, Presence, and Social Context in Facilitating Social Connectedness'. Frontiers in Psychology. 24 May 2021.

Vandenberg F., Berghman M., and Schaap J. (2020) 'The 'Lonely Raver': Music Livestreams during COVID-19 as a Hotline to Collective Consciousness?' European Societies. 14 September 2020.

Chapter

15

What always was and always will be

Ailsa Page

INTRODUCTION

Gaining wisdom and insight is one of the best things about getting older. The ability to make better decisions based on experience and gain understanding through hindsight is rewarding. I am hoping that in a couple of years we will all look back at these pandemic years and smugly reflect on our insights. In observing my world of business and marketing, many things I see have changed - but have they changed forever? Or will they, in fact, realign back to how things always were? How it looks today may not be the way it always will be. We just need to wait for the dust to settle to get the true picture. In these uncertain times, it is hard to identify the dust in the first place, and then to see if it has in reality settled. Ah well! Hindsight again will be our answer. Since we can't predict the future, let's explore in the meantime how things look today.

As a business owner for over twenty years, you start to see patterns emerge - patterns in the way your business operates, patterns in market behaviour and patterns in your behaviour as a business owner. One thing for certain that has changed in the last couple of years is there is now a lack of such predictable patterns. With the onslaught of COVID, things that once were guaranteed in business, suddenly were not. Planning that enabled predictable results was no longer a sure bet.

WHAT CHANGED

Business planning was always the key to success

A business coach mantra was 'fail to plan, plan to fail'. It has always been the case that a well-constructed business plan, if implemented, would deliver desired business outcomes. So, too, a strong marketing plan would underpin sales results. In these COVID years, plans just didn't go to plan, so to speak. Businesses that had been successful for decades were suddenly struggling with everything they had relied upon, as nothing was reliable any longer. Business knowledge and learnings built up over time did not apply anymore. A new set of rules seemed to be taking their place. But no-one could work out what the new rules were just yet. The wheels on the business bus came to a halt for the first time.

Business momentum halted

Traditionally, success in business follows an exponential curve, that is, the longer you are in business, the greater the growth. Growth is usually a little flat to start off with, but after three to five years, there is an upswing in profitability because you are leveraging business momentum. You have built up a customer base, you've achieved word of mouth referrals, have repeat customers and, ultimately, become smarter and more efficient at what you are doing. This success seems to build on success or business momentum. For some businesses, their momentum was severely hampered, which meant that the benefits built up over time started to erode and their businesses went backwards.

Same advantages for start-ups as established businesses

As noted above, benefits and advantages come from the number of years you have been in business. Due to the disruption, many established businesses that have been unable to operate for the past two years find themselves in exactly the same position as a start-up business - needing to build a new client base. Some businesses were not able to operate or were closed for such a long time that they lost their customer base completely. Imagine if you were in a relationship and your partner suggested taking a two-year break. What would be the odds of you getting back together?

Simultaneous suffering

There have been other points in time, such as post World War 2, when there were universal shortages and setbacks experienced by businesses, however, the wave of repercussions of the pandemic is new for my lifetime. My guess is that this will not be the last time that there is a shared global experience. Usually, when something negative happens to one sector, another sector benefits and vice versa, but this is usually contained to targeted industries, not widespread. The upside, because globally businesses have suffered at the same time, is there seems to be a greater understanding of some of the business suffering and disruption that has been endured.

WHAT'S CHANGED FOREVER

Online events/experiences

Out of necessity, people have had to embrace online technology to a higher degree than ever before. As a society, we are certainly more technologically competent than prior to the pandemic. Participating in online and hybrid events and managing to navigate the technology has removed a barrier for many. My ninety-year-old dad even managed to work out Zoom, just so he could stay in touch. The convenience, accessibility and cost savings online events bring, coupled with an increase in participants' comfort and acceptance, suggests they are not going away anytime soon.

Looking to government for support

Recently, I was working for the state government, offering business advice to existing businesses and start- ups. I was amazed at how many people were looking for and requesting funding to start their own business. I was surprised, as I've always seen operating your own business as requiring you to be self-determined, self-funded (or responsible for raising the funds), never expecting anyone else to make your business a success. It then dawned on me as to the 'why' this sudden shift in thinking by the public. It was the first time in my history that a government offered support to businesses without linking it to required outcomes or outputs. Advertisements promoting specific industry support funding were unleashed. I cannot help but think there is a perception shift in the minds of non-business owners that the government will help run a business. The expectation has been planted - it may, indeed, stay here forever. We will have to wait and see.

Short term planning

Have we all become more mindful, wanting to live in the present more? Or are we just scared of making plans too far into the still uncertain future? Whichever it is, it's a notable change that may be here for now or might be here to stay. Many people have experienced profound changes in the past two years - loss of freedom, a loss of dreams, time to reflect and reprioritise. This seems to have led to a change in behaviour that extends beyond personal thinking into business and buying behaviour. Lead times have shrunk and there is definitely more buying now rather than waiting. Also, the days as a consultant having your year booked out ahead of time might just be a thing of the past.

WHAT ALWAYS WAS AND ALWAYS WILL BE

Good marketing practices enable businesses to compete and continue

Change and adapting to change is the essence of good marketing. Keeping up with the needs, desires, circumstances of your target market, competitor offerings and external factors is vital if you are to stay competitive. The word 'pivot' has been given a good run in the last couple of years, but it is not a new word, nor a new business concept. Adapting to the marketplace is just what good businesses do. Businesses unable to be flexible and adapt their offering in recent times have been less successful than those that could. Good marketing practice has always given businesses an advantage. The difference is that now it is what enables businesses to survive. Restaurants that were able to provide safe online ordering, pick-up, or delivery during the last couple of years are still standing. Manufacturers able to adapt to manufacturing in-demand items like PPE or hand sanitiser increased sales. Businesses have been, collectively, put to the test during the pandemic; nevertheless, being put to the test is part of business. During other times, the test has been the Global Financial Crisis, extreme weather events, fluctuations in currency, or a change of government or legislation. We need flexible business hips, as pivoting has always been, and will remain, part of the business journey.

Business owners are the best people to steer their ship through crisis

Only you as the business owner have the capacity to navigate your way through uncertain times. You can get ideas, inspiration, and support from others, but ultimately, you as the business owner are responsible for the destination of your business. Yes, it was great here in Australia with some support for businesses from government - it made a difference, keeping businesses afloat when they could not trade, however, the government ultimately cannot take the wheel and steer your business ship. That is your job, because no one knows the waters (environment) in which you are operating, your crew (staff) and the vessel (your business) better than you. It is not helpful, nor has it ever been, to look to others to provide your business success.

Time in business is on your side

The longer you've been in business, the more resources you have at your disposal to compete. Over time, you have a greater opportunity to put something away for that rainy day - I like to call it a buffer, that is, an amount of money or certain resources in reserve, just in case you see a need. Many long-standing businesses, despite severe disruption, were better placed than newer businesses to bounce back. Positive supplier relationships that have been established, a good credit history, loyal customers, greater resilience, and experience in dealing with tough situations, are great assets to have during challenging times. In and out of pandemic experience can count.

Ailsa Page is a Fellow of the UBSS Centre for Entrepreneurship

Chapter

16

Musings on Music, Musicians, and the Metaverse

Fabian Lim

INTRODUCTION

Popping my favourite music compact disc (**CD**) into the player, the CD starts to skip, making intermittent deafening moments of silence. Finding a local repair technician specializing in CD player rebuilding was an insurmountable task, and replacing a CD player challenging, because consumer electronic stores have ceased selling CD players since CD stores have all but disappeared from the face of the island state of Singapore (although a single That CD store at the Shoppes at Marina Bay Sands still hangs on to this last vestige of a digital dinosaur medium for sale). The gradual disappearance of music CDs with other compact disc formats for media and data storage is evident in music consumerism's decline in using this type of digital media. As a result, selling one's creative musical output through sales of CDs has gradually disappeared in the last decade.

Music CDs were in the 1980s and 90s a digitized format of music that replaced analogue music recordings on cassette tape and records. Through the sales of recorded music, especially CDs, musicians could sustain themselves (Botstein, 2019), apart from music performance tours (Swanson, 2013). A little later, the advent of the digitized music coding format called MPEG-3, or mp3, popularised by music piracy used peer-to-peer sharing networks like Napster and Kazaa. As music was shared amongst users and became inherently "free for the taking", it led to revenue decline through CD sales for musicians. As music digitization developed, so, too, did new platforms to stream music, usually through a regular paid subscription or pay-per-song download on Apple Music, Spotify, Tidal, etc. Musicians who sold their music through these streaming platforms eventually realized that they were paid paltry monetary tokens from their music sales. Incredulously, Spotify's popular but controversial "freemium" subscription service only paid music creators' uploads on an average of $0.004 per stream. After significant financial losses in the 2000s, record label companies now claim to earn substantial profits from music sales through streaming platforms. My personal experience of releasing a digital EP (extended play record) of 5 instrumental song covers only garners some USD$25 every month in shared stream profits with another musician and an internet media agent. The agent streams music on various platforms, including YouTube, as playlists of song collections. Without the agent, getting sufficient plays would be even more dismal, much less to be sufficiently renumerated for the effort to record and produce the music. There appears to be no other alternative to make a living as a music creative other than performing to a live audience. Only recently, some government bodies, like the British parliament, under pressure from music artistes, began taking action. This is with the hope that music streaming business models will change and pay musicians' music uploads on streaming platforms more royalties (Sisario, 2021). Reports of paid and advertisement-supported streaming music subscriptions in 2020 had risen almost 20% to $13.4 billion, with 433 million users of paid subscriptions in 2020 (Gumuchian, 2021). But the persisting question continues to prevail: how much did musicians receive from this increase in digital music streaming?

IMPACT OF THE GLOBAL PANDEMIC

Then global pandemic hit. International music festivals ground to a halt. Global travel ceased as all international borders shut off tourists and external visitors. Within each country, lockdowns and restricted movements challenged the livelihood of all musicians. A few pre-COVID years ago, in my conversation with Jean-Paul

"Bluey" Maunick, bandleader of renowned UK jazz-funk band, *Incognito*, he mentioned that the primary way to survive as a band was to continue touring performances in international festivals and venues. The pandemic arrested all such live music performances. Closer to home, musician friends reminisce their performing experiences in China during music tours with famous singers in the pre-COVID years. With the pandemic, such international tours and work for musicians almost completely dried up. The global COVID-19 situation also meant more people stayed home and worked from home, encouraging people's reliance on video and audio recordings from home with the ease of online access (Botstein, 2019). Fans of regionally popular local artistes like *Stephanie Sun* and *Kit Chan* were still able to watch their singing idols' online, restricted-pilot performances from Singapore during the past two years of lockdowns. Will international concert tours continue after the pandemic becomes endemic? When these tours restart, will it be the same as before 2020?

WILL THINGS BE THE SAME AGAIN?

The Singapore-based consumer online survey amid the pandemic in 2020 revealed the lack of public regard for arts practitioners compared to other professions. Arts practitioners, like musicians, top the list as non-essential workers because they do not "meet the basic needs of human survival and well-being, such as food, health, safety and cleaning" (Ang & Kiew, 2020). This foreboding survey seemed to ring the death knell for many involved in the arts industry in Singapore. Many musicians, sound engineers, and others in the arts field turned to other jobs as a means of survival. Reports of the decline of live music from the pandemic were global, from China (Gu et al., 2021) to the US (Botstein, 2019). At the time of writing, the Singapore government continues taking a cautious stance towards border reopening to foreign music performances, keeping to limited seating in the audience, and allowing only a measure of local restricted public performances. Unlike many countries which have begun permitting concerts and music tours, live music performances in Singapore in pubs, hotel ballrooms, and restaurants remain prohibited. The consequential effect has been the shuttering of established live music institutions in Singapore like *Crazy Elephant* and *Wala Café Bar*, leaving regular band acts scrambling to look for alternative means of income.

LIVE STREAMED MUSIC PERFORMANCES

In mid-2020 during the pandemic, I was among the first few musicians who joined in the initial onset of live-streamed music performances sponsored by a music agent through a local community club. The viewership for the first stream of Late Night Sax hit more than five thousand views, including post-stream views by the next day, both to local and international viewers. The incredible viewership can be attributed to the first lockdown because of the novelty of watching live performances through a social media platform. A year later, the plethora of streaming shows on various platforms led to the tumbling of viewership ratings for each stream. *Streaming does not appear to be a long-lasting answer for live music performances.* Currently, a small group of musicians, especially jazz musicians, still benefit from live streaming performances through generous funding from a handful of private sponsors. But for how long will these non-profitable performances last? Philanthropic organizations are not bottomless pits of funds to support the arts forever. While musicians get paid here to stream, it was painful to find out through social media the diametric lack of similar philanthropy for public performances in the US. Until today, many renowned American jazz musicians continue their live stream performances without sponsorship, but appeal to public donations instead.

At the start of 2022, big-name bands and musicians have restarted their performance tours to make up for the lost COVID years. Everyone from *Coldplay* to the *Eagles, Katy Perry* to *Ed Sheeran,* has lined up performance tour dates in the US or Europe for the rest of the year, some even into 2023. For the big-name music artistes, the restoration of live music performances attempts to re-live pre-COVID days of global sell-out concerts, and perhaps to recoup financial losses from the two years of absence. But what about the masses of less famous local musicians? What will the future hold for these professional musicians to make a living without live music?

NFT AND NEW PERFORMANCE PLATFORMS IN THE VIRTUAL WORLD

Two new growing areas seem to provide glimmers of hope for the musician - music NFT and new performance platforms in the online virtual world or metaverse. Non-fungible tokens, or NFTs, are unique digital files existing in a blockchain as a cryptocurrency asset with verifiable ownership that can also be sold. *Kings of Leon's* first-ever music NFT album launch last year paved the way for music NFT and was met with resounding success. Musicians may finally have a chance to be impartially compensated for their creative works and retain rights to them, find new ways to capitalize on the scarcity of their products, and collaborate with other artistes (Fatemi, 2022). Music NFT with these positive attributes may be the next big thing to revolutionize the music industry.

With the metaverse looking set to explode, attending virtual reality concerts may be the rage in the near future. In these performances, musicians will perform as self-designed avatars on a ticketed global stage in a cyber world, attended avatars of a real audience. Within the metaverse, there is a fusion between real and digital environments - real-time interaction between virtual and other users. In 2021, Epic Games hosted Travis Scott in a first-ever virtual concert on their popular video game, Fortnite, where 12 million gamers stopped gaming to attend the concert. Concerts in the metaverse are not just virtual streams but "can deliver a curated immersive experience for the audience" (Roy, 2021). The virtual reality of live music in Second Life first released in 2003 may, indeed, finally become the reality of tomorrow's future in live music performance and music creation.

Fabian Lim is a lecturer at Hitmaker Global Academy and LaSalle College of the Arts. He is also a doctoral candidate at the College of Fine Arts, Boston University

REFERENCES

Ang, P., & Kiew, C. (2020, June 16). *Artists defend value of creative work to society after survey sparks debate.* The Straits Times. *https://www.straitstimes.com/lifestyle/arts/artists-defend-value-of-creative-work-to-society-after-survey-sparks-debate*

Botstein, L. (2019). *The future of music in America: The challenge of the COVID-19 pandemic.* The Musical Quarterly, 102(4). 351-360. *https://doi-org.ezproxy.bu.edu/10.1093/musqtl/gdaa007*

Fatemi, F. (2022, January 24). *Here's how NFTs could define the future of music.* Forbes. *https://www.forbes.com/sites/falonfatemi/2022/01/24/nfts-and-the-future-of-music/*

Gumuchian, M-L. (2021, March 23). *Music soothes pandemic blues as 2020 record sales hit a high note.* Reuters. *https://www.reuters.com/article/us-music-sales-ifpi-idUSKBN2BF22F*

Gu, X., Domer, N., & O'Connor, J. (2021). *The next normal: Chinese indie music in a post-COVID China.* Cultural Trends, 30(1). 63-74. *https://doi.org/10.1080/09548963.2020.1846122*

Ng, J. S. (2021, June 6). *Singaporean music conductor who became a delivery rider due to Covid-19 gets advisory role in arts charity.* Today Online. *https://www.todayonline.com/singapore/singaporean-music-conductor-who-became-delivery-rider-due-covid-19-gets-advisory-role-arts*

Roy, A. (2021, December 28). *The music industry in the metaverse: re-energized revenue streams.* XRToday. *https://www.xrtoday.com/virtual-reality/the-music-industry-in-the-metaverse-re-energised-revenue-streams/*

Sisario, B. (2021, May 2). *Musicians say streaming doesn't pay. Can the industry change?* The New York Times. *https://www.nytimes.com/2021/05/07/arts/music/streaming-music-payments.html*

Swanson, K. (2013). *A case study on Spotify: exploring perceptions of the music streaming service.* Music & Entertainment Industry Educators Association Journal, 13 (1). 207–230. *https://doi.org/10.25101/13.10*

Chapter

17

Is 2022 going to be another 'groundhog' year?

Ian Bofinger

Finishing the COVID-disrupted examinations in early December 2021, I was feeling grateful that the past 2 years of interrupted studies would be over and a return to normality would occur in 2022. What is considered "normal" for tertiary studies has also changed during the pandemic - and a return to campus doesn't necessarily spell a return to the traditional teaching paradigms of pre-2020. As such, we are left to consider the notion of whether things will ever be the same.

After almost two years of phasing in and out of remote online learning, most AMPA students and staff were looking forward to farewelling the notion of the off campus, "Zoom University" and hopeful of a return to face-to-face practical studies on campus and a sense of stability in 2022.

On December 15, 2021, the NSW government chose to phase out all lockdown measures as the state reached a double vaccination rate of 95% of the adult population. *Delta*, as well as *Omicron*, a new variant of COVID-19, decimated the state. The NSW government website data shows that COVID-19 infections went from fewer than 10 cases daily in early December 2021 to over 92,000 daily cases in early January 2022.

In AMPA's case, there was a direct correlation of these figures and the 2022 recruitment data generated from the Customer

Management System (**OAS**). In November 2021, new student information in the OAS, which is monitored daily, indicated that 2022 would see an overall growth of over 25% on 2021 student figures. Staffing plans and capital works initiatives were then designed around this encouraging data.

In late December and early January, an unexpected number of new students started to defer their offers for later in the year. International students were finding it difficult to get flights and visas, and the interstate and regional domestic students indicated that they were concerned about relocating to Sydney whilst the epidemic was appearing to be out of control.

AMPA's student demographics consist of approximately 10% international, 15% interstate, 35% regional and only 40% Sydney metropolitan. The impact on approximately 60% of the new and returning student population not permanently based in Sydney was significant.

Continuing students from Western Australia and Queensland stated that they would rather stay online due to the uncertainty of return travel communicated by the state premiers. New students chose to defer until Trimester 2, 2022. As ABC News reported, "Western Australia has delayed its planned border reopening indefinitely as the rest of the country grapples with the greatest spread of COVID-19 since the pandemic began. Premier Mark McGowan said the revised hard border would come with more exemptions for compassionate reasons. However, he warned further restrictions would be considered over the next month as the state reviews the impact of the Omicron variant in the eastern states. The changes, due to start from February 5, have dashed the hopes of families and friends hoping to reunite after being separated by some of the toughest border controls in Australia."

AMPA's regional students, who had relocated to Sydney for the 2021 academic year, have mostly returned to on-campus face-to-face studies in 2022, but many of the potential new students have chosen to defer their studies rather than access the hybrid teaching models. Anecdotal data recorded by the recruitment team indicated that after 2 years of Zoom-based studies to complete their NSW High School Certificate (**HSC**), the thought of commencing their tertiary music and dance studies online was not desirable, but the notion of relocating to Sydney during the pandemic as reported daily on the news was equally unacceptable for many students and their families.

Instead of preparing for a return to on-campus studies for 2022, AMPA staff were reminded of the 1993 movie "Groundhog Day" in which Bill Murray portrays Phil Connors, a cynical television weatherman covering the annual Groundhog Day event in Punxsutawney, Pennsylvania, who becomes trapped in a time loop, forcing him to relive February 2nd repeatedly. Every day starts the same way: an alarm clock changes from 5:59 to 6 a.m. The radio plays Sonny and Cher singing, "I Got You Babe". Wake up, do the same things, go nowhere, go to bed… This was reminiscent of our tertiary life in 2020 and 2021, but were we heading back to this exclusively remote, off-campus study model once more in 2022?

In August 2020, a report produced by Ernst & Young Global predicted the number of international students in Australia would never return to its 2019 levels. Instead, it predicted a total revenue loss of $6bn by 2030. The shortfall could force the closure or merger of smaller institutions and would mean 50% of non-research staff would be out of work.

Ernst & Young's global head of education, Catherine Friday, said the pandemic had "exposed the overreliance on on-campus learning and international students in Australia's higher education system". This generalised notion appears to be true for many tertiary degrees, but the benefits of on-campus practical studies in music and dance is contradictory to this statement. The individual, personalised mentor relationships that are fostered in the tertiary performing arts training have been almost impossible to replicate in the hybrid online models that were utilised to deliver the practical units during 2020 and 2021. The experience gained by being a part of an ensemble in a professional dance studio or from performing music on the stage under lights and industry standard sound, compared to that of working with a laptop in the student's garage or lounge room, can't be underestimated.

During the pandemic, AMPA had the opportunity to develop some high-quality online materials for the exclusively academic units such as the Music History stream. In these units, the structured preparation of all of the multimedia prepared for the online delivery, such as in-house recorded videos, commercial video segments, music scores, audio recordings and historically significant archival materials, has further enhanced the student learning experience. This has also reduced the on-campus study load to only 3 days/week for each student and has further minimised the risk of travelling to campus on public transport.

As Friday (2021) notes, "There is so much financial strain in the sector right now and such uncertainty about ongoing income and revenue streams that it's reasonable to suspect that there might be university closures or some sort of merger activity in the market."

While it will take time, AMPA continues to slowly lure back students from overseas. As Jackson (2022) states, "We have reached a milestone with the reopening of our borders, but the sector will take time to recover."

Australian universities are hoping the return of international students and face-to-face learning will help the decimated sector "snap back" from COVID restrictions, but some are warning the industry is in a perilous position. Since the pandemic, the number of international student visa holders has fallen by 205,854 - or 33.5% - with the sector losing at least $1.8bn in revenue in the first year alone, according to Universities Australia.

The full picture for enrolment and commencement numbers for both international and domestic students will not be known until March 2022, but the minister for immigration, Alex Hawke, announced that since late November 2021, a total of 56,000 international students have arrived in Australia. He also states that demand for Australian study visas has been particularly strong, in recent months, with more than 50,000 overseas student visa lodgements since late 2021. Visa grants to international students are flowing as a result of the minister directing the department to allocate additional resources to processing the visas of international students.

In the movie, 'Groundhog Day', Phil uses his predicament to grow as a person. He takes up French, ice sculpting and even piano. The good news is that, by now, we are getting better at taking life a day at a time and maybe there is still hope for tertiary studies in the Performing Arts.

Thankfully, with a mix of low attrition and late registrations, AMPA has been able to begin 2022 with a viable student cohort. The year has also begun with the hybrid model of both on-campus and online studies, as originally planned. This has also been in part possible due to the decline in the daily NSW COVID-19 infection numbers. It now looks as though 2022 will not be a repeat of the lockdowns of the past 2 years. Instead, the positive developments that have been gained from adversity in the realms of hybrid models of study will continue to enhance the learning experience of the students at AMPA.

Professor Ian Bofinger is the Executive Dean and CEO of AMPA, the Australian Academy of Music and Performing Arts.

References

Hawke, A. 2022 *Australia welcomes return of international students and backpackers https://minister.homeaffairs.gov.au/AlexHawke/Pages/australia-welcomes-return-of-international-students-and-backpackers.aspx*

Higher Education Educator, 2021 *Australia NSW to welcome back some international students https://www.theeducatoronline.com/k12/news/nsw-to-welcome-back-some-international-students/278777*

Friday, C. 2021 *University Disruption Will Continue Beyond COVID-19 https://www.ey.com/en_au/covid-19/university-disruption-will-continue-beyond-covid-19*

Jackson, C. 2022 *'Looking down the barrel': Australian universities face nervous future post-Covid https://www.theguardian.com/australia-news/2022/jan/30/looking-down-the-barrel-australian-universities-face-nervous-future-post-covid*

JHU CSSE COVID-19 Data *https://www.nsw.gov.au/covid-19*

Motherwell, S. (2022) *Here's who can enter WA after February 5 and what they need to do after arriving https://www.abc.net.au/news/2022-01-21/wa-hard-border-restrictions-approved-traveller-list/100772308*

Chapter

18

The economy will never be the same again – or will it?

Om Huvanandana

INTRODUCTION

Countries all over the world have been dealing with the coronavirus pandemic, including the economic implications of COVID-19, since 2019. The pandemic has brought with it, not only, a killing virus, but also a stand-still in people's routine daily lives, the need for social distancing, disrupted economic transactions, and anti-political movements against public policy.

All these changes will result in a new order of social behaviour, and the objective of this paper is to respond to a question, *Things will never be the same - or will they?*

From a 'bird's-eye' view, we can gain a perspective and respond to the impact by looking at major variants of society, namely, political, economic, and social change. As is evidenced in the media, all variants are subject to change in one form or the other, not only locally, but also globally.

For example, a policy to close down the transportation system in one country will stop the movement of goods and services, raw materials, labour and tourists, to other countries. This action will have a significant adverse effect on the national political, economic and social environment of both countries.

Therefore, it is useful to look, primarily, at the pandemic's impact on the economy, because it instantly and directly affects the people at large, and then, analyse whether the result will be things never being the same again.

AN ANALYSIS

The analysis looks at 4 countries - Indonesia, Thailand, Vietnam, and Singapore - as they are considered as having, together, a significant share of ASEAN Gross Domestic Product (**GDP**). Whatever happened to these countries by way of impact was to have strong repercussions on other ASEAN member countries and the region at large.

Three areas were analysed - first, the impact on GDP; second, public policy intervention; and finally, if the economy would ever be the same again.

IMPACT ON GDP

The Figure (below) shows clear evidence that COVID-19 caused a significant drop in the value of goods and services in the order of magnitude from Thailand, Singapore, and Indonesia, with the exception of Vietnam which shows, in fact, a positive growth; interestingly, Vietnam could have achieved more than 10% growth rate without COVID-19 interference.

Further to this, Singapore, and Thailand each registered the biggest slowdown in their economies, followed by Indonesia, with Vietnam registering an opportunity loss. Singapore and Thailand share similar economic structures, with a heavy reliance on international trade, with the sum of export and import value more than 100 percent of GDP.

GDP Growth 2019-2021

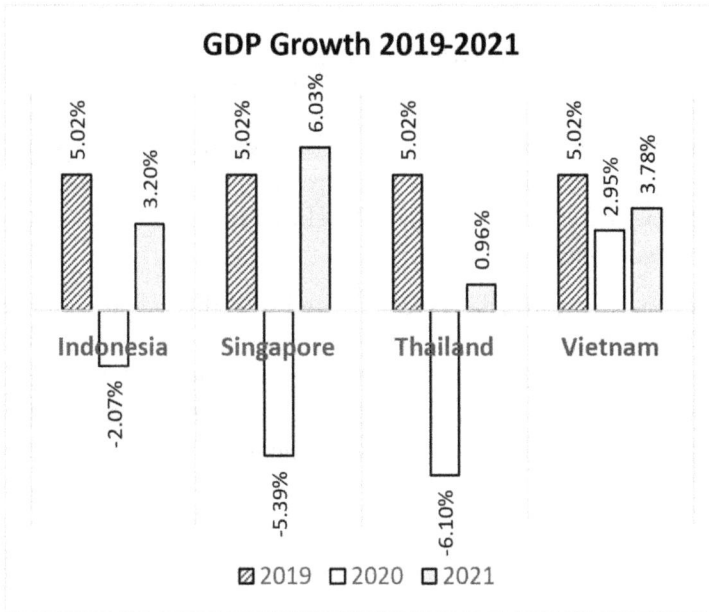

Figure 4 - Yamungkoon, O, N. (2021), Comparison of Four ASEAN countries' GDP, (UBSS, MBA)

BACKGROUND OF THE ECONOMY DURING COVID-19

COVID-19 has had a huge economic impact on Singapore and Thailand in particular. Those industries that rely on international travel, such as air transportation, lodging, and other tourism-related industries, have been the hardest hit. Domestic consumption has been cut back as a result of increasingly tougher social distance regulations, which has had a negative impact on consumer-onsite sectors, such as retail and food services.

Outward-oriented industries, such as manufacturing and wholesale commerce, have been hit by a drop in external demand, and supply chain disruptions, while domestically oriented sectors, such as construction and real estate, have been hit by negative spill overs from the domestic economy.

With the surge in demand for online commerce and services, however, there are some bright spots in the economy (Saw, Lin, & Jie, 2020). 'Things will never be the same' as online comes into the market.

Similar adverse impacts in Indonesia and Vietnam from the perspective of reduced trading activities as a result of social distancing measures and 'Work From Home' policies can be noted.

But Indonesia is a big country with a large GDP, and a population with a large proportion still in the provinces, so, the domestic market was better able to absorb the shock from COVID-19 than Thailand and Singapore.

Vietnam, as a country, is well disciplined, and this helped contain the spread of COVID-19 initially, or at least in early 2020. In addition, Vietnam has an increasing consumer group, given its industrialization, with continuing direct foreign investment inflow, resulting in the continuity of its economic growth.

PUBLIC POLICY

The coordination of fiscal and monetary policy is a necessary condition for macroeconomic stability and long-term economic growth (Chugunov, et al, 2021). Fiscal policy can be defined as the process by which the government influences the economy through spending and taxation, with the primary goal of influencing the level and rate of growth of aggregate demand, employment, and output.

Monetary policy, on the other hand, covers the use of 'mean' with the goal of regulating the value, supply, and cost of money - in accordance with the desired level of economic activity. In order to mitigate the adverse effects of COVID-19 on employment and, most importantly, on the national income, the government – instead of the private and the export sectors - must spend money.

The populist policy, or cash hand-out, was implemented, with a consequence of a budget deficit, and an increasing national debt.

The money can support the national expenditure in the short run, but, as John Maynard Keynes once argued, during the Great Depression of 1930, the government must act immediately - it needs to take action.

"In the long run, we are All Dead." (Rinchakorn, 2022) Let us consider this.

The monetary policy must support the fiscal populist policy by making money available for the private sector credit ease, and to support the fiscal policy in times of an epidemic. All these policies will result in a loosening of disciplinary measures and begin the new order of the public policy that conserves rather than constructs the nation.

Things will never be the same again - will they?

THE ECONOMY WILL NEVER BE THE SAME

The reduction in the rate of GDP growth resulted in the change of the economy structure, especially in terms of an export income associated with tourism, logistics and trading services.

Thailand will lose a significant share of foreign tourism, especially from China. More *online* tourism businesses, though, will grow and replace the traditional tour business providers.

The industrial sector will also shift from one country to another within ASEAN, from Thailand to Indonesia and Vietnam, as evidenced by the flow of a foreign direct investment.

The adjustment is a Zero-Sum Game, where one country gains at the expense of the others. Therefore, the economy will never be the same - both in terms of consumer behaviour and the producer's entrepreneurial spirit.

But what is happening has been long witnessed by Joseph Schumpeter, who coined the term, "The Creative Destruction", to mean better products and services keep on coming to replace the existing ones.

And, so, the creative destruction will be the same - won't it.

Adjunct Professor Om Huvanandana is a Fellow of the UBSS Centre for Scholarship and Research

REFERENCES

BANK, W. (2021, October. *https://www.worldbank.org/*. Retrieved from *https://www.worldbank.org/en/country/indonesia/overview#1*

Chugunov. (2021), *Macro Stability and Economic Growth.* ECONOMICS, T. (2021). https://tradingeconomics.com. Retrieved from *https://tradingeconomics.com/thailand/interest-rate*GROUP

W. B. (2020). *COVID-19 Policy Response Notes of Vietnam.* Ho, G. (2020). *https://www.straitstimes.com.* Retrieved from *https://www.straitstimes.com/singapore/government-mounting-fiscal-firepower-fighting-covid-19-number-one-job-dpm-heng*

News, V. N. (2021) *https://vietnamnews.vn/* Retrieved from *https://vietnamnews.vn/economy/592363/covid-19-highlights-need-for-economic restructuring.html*

Rinchakorn. (2022). *https://www.gotoknow.org/posts/484062*

Saw, C., Lin, J., & Jie, W. Y. (2020). *Economic Survey of Singapore First Quarter 2020. Impact of the COVID-19 Pandemic on the Singapore Economy.*

Suwannasopon, T. (2021, November 30). *Economics MCR001. Vietnam economics: Monetary and future trend after Covid-19.*

TIMES, T. B. (2021). *https://www.businesstimes.com.sg/hub/.* Retrieved from *https://www.businesstimes.com.sg/hub/indonesia-76th-independence-day/indonesian-governments-strategies-in-response-to-covid-19*

Vogado, S. (2021). *https://www.focus-economics.com/.* Retrieved from *https://www.focus-economics.com/countries/thailand/news/fiscal/government-announces-mildly-expansionary-fy-2021-budget-amid-ongoing*

Wu, A. M. (2021, June). *https://www.csc.gov.sg/.* Retrieved from *https://www.csc.gov.sg/articles/fiscal-responses-to-covid-19-in-singapore-and-hong-kong*

Yamungkoon,O.N. (2021). *Comparison of four ASEAN countries GDP, during Covid-19, 2019-2021*

Chapter

19

Hybrid learning for post COVID-19 – why it matters

Richard Xi

INTRODUCTION

It is unfortunate that COVID-19 has generated enormous challenges for higher education institutions (**HEIs**), particularly for those whose revenue relies heavily upon international students. These institutions were further challenged, thanks to the dramatic decline of enrolment numbers as a result of border closures, various restrictions on international mobility, and the government's rules and policies with regard to national safety concerns. Indeed, it is also a challenge for international students who are faced with the constant changing conditions and an uncertain future, as far as pursuing their dream of gaining an Australian higher education degree is concerned. With the more recent development of COVID-19 and the government's initiative of reopening borders, it is the time to plan a sustainable learning model that can best satisfy international students' needs and help HEIs' position in gaining the competitive advantages in the global market for the post COVID-19 future. According to various surveys which asked students about their preferences for staying online or returning to face-to-face (**F2F**) course delivery, most students indicated they would like to keep the current online learning model, confirming a strong need for a workable and effective hybrid solution for HEIs to consider in the context of post COVID-19 (Whateley 2021; Miroshnikov 2021).

WHAT WE KNOW ABOUT HYBRID LEARNING

Things are not, and will never be, the same as a result of the changes caused by the global COVID-19 pandemic. The world is entering a hybrid era on a scale and to a degree we never expected, and one we have never experienced before: hybrid teaching and learning for schools and students, hybrid working for office workers (in office and working from home), and hybrid socialising for people engaging and attending social events and activities. For example, I recently attended a social event - a memorial service - online (due to COVID-19 restriction rule), together with a group of people gathered on site, and the service was carried out in a hybrid mode, simultaneously.

The definition of hybrid learning, however, is often confused with blended learning, due to the existence of ambiguity, or we might say, because of the absence of clear criteria and clarification. As such, it makes it difficult to distinguish one from the other, as they both adopt a combination of F2F and online learning components. For example, one of the most popular definitions is from Graham (2006) who defines blended learning as the system that combines "face-to-face instruction with computer-mediated instruction". Friesen (2012) further suggests that blended learning combines internet and digital media with established classroom forms that require the physical co-presence of teacher and students. Hall and Davison (2007) describe hybrid learning as combining some of the features of a traditionally taught class with access to online learning tools. So, it is difficult to draw an analogy between blended learning and hybrid learning in order to understand a unique characteristic which pertains to both - the two different approaches share the common concepts, online and F2F, and inevitably, there is confusion, along with misunderstanding. It seems, the two concepts are categorised by one definition, and so, in practice, hybrid and blended become interchangeable, depending upon the context and purpose of delivery.

WHAT DO WE MEAN BY HYBRID LEARNING?

Since the post COVID-19 era is within our sights, and the border reopening is imminent, a clear and workable hybrid learning mode should be considered as a priority and one of the key factors in seeking an institution's competitive advantages in the context of a highly competitive international education market. A clear understanding of hybrid learning must be established as a foundation to help higher education providers in the planning and developing of a hybrid delivery mode fit to accommodate international students, both onshore and offshore in the post COVID era.

To distinguish the concept of hybrid delivery from blended delivery, Whateley (2021) pointed out that the 'hybrid delivery is a simultaneous activity requiring no more preparation or time than F2F teaching', as both modes (online and F2F) are delivered simultaneously, and it is for the student to choose the mode that suits them the best. There are three key elements here, I would suggest, which contribute to the uniqueness of hybrid learning in terms of time, space, and the student's autonomy:

Time

Hybrid delivery is synchronised - lecturer presents and delivers the content from the classroom in front of the students who either attend F2F in the classroom or participate in the same class through online (facilitated with information communication technology (ICT), for example, video, audio, and other cyber components) at the same time. There is no difference between F2F attendants and online participants with regard to lecture delivery, class activities, intercommunications, and interactions between lecturers and students, and between students in two different settings. The characteristic of synchronicity of the hybrid learning mode could also provide the workable solution of delivering courses to the students in what we might call the multi-campus or 'satellite-campus', where utilising an institution's limited resources (staff, space, finance, and administration etc.) can be done so effectively and efficiently.

Space

Regardless of geographical aspect, being close to school or attending from a remote place, being onshore or offshore, there is simply no 'space' restriction for hybrid learning, thanks to digital technology pushing internet speed to its limit and mobile technology bridging the spatial distance. Basically, this is a 'hybrid classroom', where a teacher delivers their subject content from a technology-equipped classroom to students who either physically attend the class (F2F) or take part online in a remote virtual 'classroom' (for example, in any room of their home place, worksite, on public transport or even inside of a parked car). Furthermore, there is no restriction upon the students with a virtual and mobile 'classroom', regardless of the geographical barrier and physical distance. It is digital and cyber technology that have made this possible.

Student's Autonomy

The hybrid learning mode will significantly enrich the concept of student-centred learning in their journey to complete a higher education degree in Australia, particularly from the perspective of international students. It gives freedom and power to students to take charge of their own learning process, and students can exercise their choice to either participate on campus in a F2F class or online. It certainly enhances a student's engagement as it 'requires a psychological investment on the part of the learner as well as persistence in understanding the learning task' (Blakey, 2015). The freedom and power derived from hybrid learning may increase international students' satisfaction, in particular in terms of having more flexibility in allocating their time and budget, in balancing their commitment to study, work, family, and other social activities, when compared with a fully online mode or fully F2F on campus mode. The exercising of a student's autonomy also provides international students with the mix of socialising with their peers either on campus or online.

The co-existence of F2F and online helps students to build on their capacity to meet the need of a sense of belonging to their class and school community. This is especially important to international students who live and study in a foreign country where there is a totally new cultural environment - having a variety of ways of communicating and socialising with their classmates can contribute to an enjoyable learning experience. This, in turn, is likely to enhance a student's psychological willingness to actively engage in their learning, both in class and outside of campus.

HYBRID LEARNING AND STUDENT LEARNING EXPERIENCE

The benefits and opportunities that hybrid learning can generate are obvious and encouraging from the perspective of international students. The co-existence of opportunities and challenges for hybrid learning in the future has attracted popular attention from academics and other stakeholders. It has triggered a broad discussion and includes the various perspectives of the academics and management who shed light on technology, as well as pedagogy, etc., however, it is also worth examining how the hybrid model contributes to students gaining positive outcomes from their learning experience during and post implementation.

It is suggested that a positive student experience heavily relies upon a highly collaborative effort, from the academics through to administration, alongside IT, student services, and management of the organization, each with a strong customer focused initiative. The hybrid method is best when it can facilitate students working comfortably with the key technology applications, particularly as far as the institution's learning management system and learning platforms are concerned. Online/F2F lectures, assessments, including exams, tests, group assignments, and quizzes etc., where Moodle, Blackboard, and other systems are accessible, are integral to the success of the hybrid delivery mode. It is also crucial that students are well aware of the basic requirement of technology readiness (including a reliable computer, internet speed, web-tech, common/personal technic know-how, etc.), especially the first-year international student who finds themselves in a completely new environment.

HEIs and students have experienced rapid changes and are facing considerable challenges driven by the COVID-19 pandemic. There is no going back to the traditional, more than a century-old learning model and yesterday's 'status quo' in the hope of meeting the future challenges of the post COVID-19 era, all in the context of the world of digitalization and mobilization. Any challenge comes with opportunity, and hybrid learning is not an exception. It doesn't matter what the challenge is and how many there are - what matters most is how we manage to transform the challenge into opportunity and convert opportunity to success.

Richard Xi is an assistant professor and a senior postgraduate co-ordinator at UBSS

REFERENCES

Blakey, C. & Major, C. 2019, 'Student Perceptions of Engagement in Online Course: An Exploratory Study', Online Journal of Distance Learning Administration, vol. XXII, no. 4., *https://www.westga.edu/~distance/ojdla/winter224/blakeymajor224.html*

Friesen, N., 2012. Defining blended learning. Learning Spaces. *https://www.normfriesen.info/papers/Defining_Blended_Learning_NF.pdf*

Graham, C. R. (2006). Blended learning systems: Definition, current trends, and future directions. In C. J. Bonk & C. R. Graham (Eds.), The handbook of blended learning: Global perspectives, local designs (pp. 3-21). San Francisco: Pfeiffer.

Hall, H., & Davison, B. (2007). Social software as support in hybrid learning environment: The value of the blog as a tool for reflective learning and peer support. *https://www.napier.ac.uk/~/media/worktribe/output-238428/social-software-as-support-in-hybrid-learning-environments-the-value-of-the-blog-as-a.pdf*

Mirroshnikov, G. (2021). Education's Hybrid Future: What We Know from Research. *https://campustechnology.com/articles/2021/07/21/educations-hybrid-future-what-we-know-from-research.aspx*

Whateley, G. (2021). What is meant by 'hybrid' delivery and how does it work in higher education? *https://www.ubss.edu.au/media/2670/understanding-hybrid-delivery.pdf*

Chapter

20

Some Things Stay the Same

Tom O'Connor

INTRODUCTION

If we were to look at curriculum as the "product" in an educational enterprise, then the timetable represents the "delivery" of that product. So, the development of a timetable in any educational institution is of critical importance, and it is no surprise then, that the development of a timetable has also been affected by the events of the last two years.

TIMETABLING

Timetabling in a normal year is a complex undertaking, but it is far more difficult in times of change and pressure. The construction of a timetable in a school setting means organizing a range of limited resources - the students, teachers, time, and spaces. Quite some time before COVID-19, I was responsible for the development of a timetable for amalgamating schools. Throughout the 1990s in Victoria, there was a widespread move to amalgamate smaller schools in response to demographic changes across the state. This affected government and Catholic schools which were effectively part of a "system", and during this time of transition, I became Deputy Principal for Curriculum in a school that, after amalgamating three smaller schools within a six-month period in 1996, would become a three-campus, 1500-student operation. There was a neat synergy across the three, with one school having a surplus of space and some good technical facilities, a second school presenting with high numbers and desperately short of space, while the third, one kilometre away, had a cash surplus. In project management terms, the project had been initiated by the "system" authorities, with a deadline set for February 2nd.

PROJECT MANAGEMENT

In the waterfall model of project management, several successive steps - one depending on the other - were necessary before the timetable could be developed. First, curriculum leaders were to be appointed for all areas in order to manage the process. This was time-consuming, but not as time-consuming as merging the three separate curriculums into one comprehensive program. The newly appointed curriculum leaders and I had to work through the many issues that surfaced, some issues resolved more quickly than others. Staff were wedded to their previous practice, but part of the brief for the new entity was to provide increased opportunity for all students. On the one hand, while arguments raged about what novels were suitable for girls, a quick decision was made that boys would study Fabric (what used to be called Sewing), while girls would study Woodwork. This decision created the need for a shuttlebus and the transport of students throughout the day from one campus to another - just one example of a multitude of decisions that had to be made before a timetable could be constructed. In effect, each of these decisions created many micro-projects that needed to be managed along the way. Each independent choice impacted on resources and personnel, and so, during planning, what may have been a possible allocation of resources in one week, would be rendered impossible by another decision. So, it became clear that all decisions, that is all the data, needed to be in place before the timetable could be executed.

The three smaller schools did not formally conclude operations until the end of the school year in the December. There were formalities surrounding the closures and farewelling of staff, and sensitive personnel matters that needed to be allowed to proceed, affording the individuals respect for their contributions. So, while planning decisions had been made, no work on the actual timetable could take place. What followed was the Christmas-New Year break and pre-planned holidays. The Daily Organiser (DO) who was working on the timetable with me arrived January 16, giving us two weeks to have everything regarding timetabling ready. Like many projects, this amalgamation had critics, with people, I dare say, waiting for chaos to ensue. Nevertheless, as far as the new entity was concerned, a great deal of prestige and personal integrity rested on its completion. A sentence from the movie 'Apollo 13', was often quoted, "Failure is not an option". Needless to say, there was a great deal of pressure.

TIMETABLING TOOL

The tool we were using was a sophisticated timetabling program developed locally. The first step was data entry which was an exacting process in itself. All the restrictions, such as part time staff and specialist room usage, were to be entered first, followed by staff names and their teaching areas, and then class sizes and student names and subjects. In future years, most of the data would rollover, but the initial phase meant entering everything. One week was dedicated to this task, leaving one other week to complete the timetable. Even the most sophisticated software can only complete 90% of a timetable. Every school is different, and, I hasten to add, a drama or music class cannot be scheduled in a room beside a silent reading English class. Certain leadership staff members were to be allocated Period 1 'free' each day in order to attend to student needs and, indeed, the list goes on. Procedure would have it that the program is run, and a draft timetable is produced along with a table of resources, despite the staff and/ or student allocation clashes that, at this point in the process, remain unresolved.

Projects occur within a human environment, and, as such, there are impacts. By the last week of a stifling January, the DO and I were working 18 to 20-hour days and getting a few hours' sleep in the staff room. The DO's wife was in the eighth month of her pregnancy and had moved into the sick bay at the school to be near him, in case the baby would not wait! Meanwhile, work continued. The process was one of iteration. Fixing one or two problems at a time and re-running the program, making sure the changes did not cause any more issues required a method of controlling and monitoring any progress. As each problem was revealed, we took time to think it through, canvas possible solutions, input the desired response and run the program again. Perhaps not unexpectedly, as the end of the project drew near, each remaining problem became much more complicated, difficult, and time-consuming. The night of February 1 into February 2 was very warm and muggy. We sat outside the school reception building while the DO's wife brought coffee to us. At about 3am, a police car pulled up and two officers walked in and asked us what we were doing. The DO, unmoved, said, "Having a smoke." I intervened to explain the situation when the DO's wife appeared. Taken aback, she interjected and asked if they wanted a coffee. This was not something these officers came across every day, and it seems they decided our situation was too bizarre to be a manufactured one and left.

At around 5am, we finished and began printing the individual timetables and class lists. At 6.45am, the paperwork was taken to the various administration offices, where the secretaries who began their workday at 7.30 would begin distribution. At 8.45 on February 2, the new school commenced with a functioning timetable.

NEW AND DIFFERENT SET OF CHALLENGES

Jump to February 2020. I am managing eight schools, delivering VCE across China. The international staff have left for the Lunar New Year holiday, travelling home to countries which include Trinidad and Tobago, Poland, the Ukraine and New Zealand, with some to visit relatives in Japan. Meanwhile, in China, where millions are travelling domestically, COVID is spreading rapidly and lockdowns are being instituted, first in Wuhan and then in various other cities. Elsewhere (O'Connor 2022), I have described the pivot to online learning that took place in this scenario. The delivery of resources - that is, the timetabling - took on a completely different set of challenges. The normal class setting of teacher and students in a room disappeared. The students were all at home in China in what turned out to be an extended lockdown, while teachers were stranded in various countries across the planet. With the decision to go to online learning, there had to be a new approach to timetabling. School resumed in the last week of February and a structure had to be in place for classes to start. The immovable factor was over 500 students in China, while the other constant was the mobile phone, with all students owning one. So, that screen would in effect become the learning portal. For each day we needed to provide six hours of online teaching. By examining the different time zones and negotiating with teachers, a class schedule was prepared, with some teachers working at 4am in their local time. It was not physically possible, however, to provide constant "in person" online learning, therefore, some sessions were recorded and slotted in during the day. In addition, in Melbourne, a series of online classes was recorded, to be used when the inevitable illness presented, or problem occurred in any of the locations where teachers found themselves. The outcome meant school commenced, but it was a taxing time for all concerned.

INNOVATIVE SOLUTIONS TO PROBLEMS ENCOUNTERED

The COVID-19 pandemic has produced some innovative solutions to problems. The essentials of secondary school timetabling remain the same: putting students into a space where a teacher can communicate with them at a scheduled time. There have been major changes to the concept of teaching - first has been the concept of asynchronous classes, where recorded lessons are used during a part of the daily schedule, but are also available "out of hours", so the notion of when school happens is more fluid; the second is the removal of the need to be in one physical space. The electronic classroom has become a viable option, and the location of teachers and students is in some ways secondary - as long as there is an internet connection, there is teaching. While the basics of timetabling have not changed, the parameters have expanded, reinventing schooling and, in doing so, creating far greater demands on the lonely timetable.

Adjunct Professor Tom O'Connor is currently a Secondary/Higher Education Consultant, a Member of the UBSS Academic Senate and Fellow of the UBSS Centre for Scholarship and Research

Chapter

21

Competing in the post COVID-19 world - Is it different or just faster than before?

Andy Wong

THE CHALLENGING WORLD

Before the onset of the pandemic in 2019, the global society faced ongoing, seemingly endless, problems. Rising sea levels due to the melting of the ice in the north-pole, rising temperatures due to pollution, and the greenhouse effect, where the depleting food resources as a result of the increasing population, together, had us wondering about the environmental crisis. Indeed, our attention, whether on the business environment, where industries have been disrupted by the evolution of technology, the automation of work processes which have led to the redundancies of human labour, rising technology companies taking over the world as Unicorns, or the disruption on the vertical chain of many businesses across the globe, was to be redirected. In came the COVID-19 pandemic.

The rise of the modern world, two years into the third decade of the twenty-first century, demands that we consider this crisis we now face in light of the past, and ask ourselves if there are any differences. Many say COVID-19 changed the world. We hear this every day - in the news, journal articles, newspapers, from friends, relatives, advocates, et cetera. I would say this is another disruption on a significant scale. But has it ever happened before? The answer is yes, but it seems the 1918 – 1920 H1N1 Influenza A virus has been all but forgotten. This greatest flu infected one billion people and killed approximately one hundred million. It is worth mentioning here that perhaps crises can never be avoided, and that the one constant is we are surrounded by imminent threats from nature and, no doubt, the business environment. As a result of COVID-19, we have seen many businesses cease to exist; in contrast, many others have propelled exponentially. So let us focus on the business environment for a moment. If we face reality, it becomes clear a company must remain competitive by frequently reviewing its strategy against the macro and micro business environment, closely monitoring its SWOT model, analysing, and reviewing its core competencies to ensure the business remains relevant in the industry.

THE CATALYST

Arun Sundararajan, NYU Stern School of Business professor said, "Crisis can be a catalyst or can speed up changes that are on the way, and it can almost serve as an accelerant." (Sundararajan. A, 2021)

The COVID-19 pandemic can be said to have spurred the growth of the consumer base for technology companies and to have set the groundwork for start-ups to prove the value of their product and services, and indeed, their business model. In early 2016, I joined See Chic, a French-founded eyecare e-commerce company, as the finance director. As a start-up, See Chic, along with many other tech-companies, rented a co-sharing space in the CBD district. Among us was an online supermarket company, RedMart (before the acquisition by Alibaba), a telehealth services company and many more. Back then, RedMart struggled to meet sales targets because consumers were not convinced of purchasing fresh goods online; at least, I was not confident then. Telehealth also had a problem convincing both the consumer and the regulators of their online health screening process. See Chic and Telehealth each faced an issue with the supply chain and the regulators because of the mandatory prescription required before customers purchase products, in our case, contact lenses, online. The local Eyecare

Association in Singapore imposed a sanction that restricted See Chic from accessing the supplies in Singapore. Due to its e-commerce nature, however, See Chic managed to obtain supplies and fulfil orders from Hong Kong, dropping or shipping to our customers' homes. What See Chic did was focus on the delivery channel of its products and services. Put simply, the process involves the booking and conducting of professional mobile home-to-home optometry services by a qualified optometrist. Upon receiving the prescription, customers are given a discount voucher to purchase their contact lenses at the See Chic e-commerce enabled website. Once the order is placed, the supplier in Hong Kong sends the products to the warehouse, where it is packed and shipped directly from Hong Kong to the home of the customers in Singapore, the completion of an order taking less than one week. Within a year, See Chic was listed in the Euromonitor as one of the emerging eyewear retailing concepts in Asia Pacific.

> "SeeChic.com, an online eyewear retailer is seen as a game changer in the eyewear industry in Asia Pacific. Started in late 2015, See Chic is based in Singapore, but products are shipped to 10 countries in Asia." (Euromonitor, 2016)

In the case of See Chic, I've witnessed the team's ability to execute a brilliant strategy to resolve a business model crisis. Failing this, the company would not have been able to run its business at all.

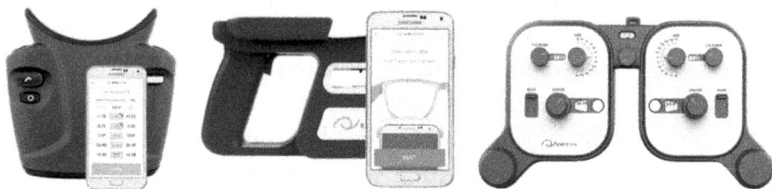

Figure 5 - Mobile Eye Test Devices
Source: Carl Zeiss AG and Eyenetra

POST-COVID IN THE EDUCATION INDUSTRY

Analysts predicted a US$350 billion market valuation for the EdTech industry by 2025, before the inception of COVID-19. Change, it seems, is not always detrimental. During the pandemic, the education industry was caught with an unprecedented change in terms of how courses were delivered and managed. Many schools, ranging from K-12 to stand-alone secondary schools and universities, were forced into remote learning. The rapid move to digitalise the learning environment, whilst challenging, contributed to the growth of a few areas:

1. Increased development and usage of digital teaching materials. In Singapore, a semi-private institution, such as St. Joseph Institution (**SJI**), adopted the use of Classin, an integrated school and learning management system, as one of its teaching resources. Teachers at SJI developed interactive content that promotes engagement and critical thinking, using the concept of Edutainment via the Classin Webapp.
2. Increased mobile applications in higher education institutions promoted socialisation within the school communities, improved communication, and promoted mobile learning.
3. Rapid digital transformation, especially in the AI development in machine learning in robotics, contact tracing and remote learning capability, saw government focusing on the development of AI, and with limited human contact during the COVID period, machines were programmed to work with limited human interference.
4. There was a rise in demand for graduate learning content for working adults and an increase in continuous professional skills upgrading. Mass Open Online Course (**MOOC**) providers, such as Coursera, saw an increase in users to 189 million in 2021.
5. There was a move into the mixed, virtual, and augmented reality to create a community-based metaverse for education, where students attend a controlled environment, especially in higher education. Somniumspace, The SandBox, and Decentraland were created, offering an

immersive experience, complete with space, community, market places for trade and business and the ownership of digital assets, such as, virtual land, avatar, digital attire, et cetera.

Investors are now convinced of the potential development in the online education industry. Online or remote learning is no longer limited to e-learning or mobile-learning, blended or hybrid mode, as the world has moved into mixed reality and the metaverse.

Give this good thought for a moment - before the pandemic, more than twenty years ago, technology existed. Lucus, my fourteen-year-old son, has recently become the centre of my discussion with my wife in relation to his time spent on Roblox, now a 39-billion-dollar IPO company (valued in March 2021). Lucus has been playing Roblox for four to five years at least. I recalled, in conversation, that I had never played any games that lasted so long, and that the last time I played was when I played the RPG Red Alert, and this had lasted for a month. The point is that Lucus is not just playing games, he is living another life in the metaverse. He has a meta identity, avatar, virtual assets, and virtual friends he has not met in the real world. All this happened before the pandemic - twenty years ago there was SIM city, a 3-D interactive game featuring the inception of the metaverse.

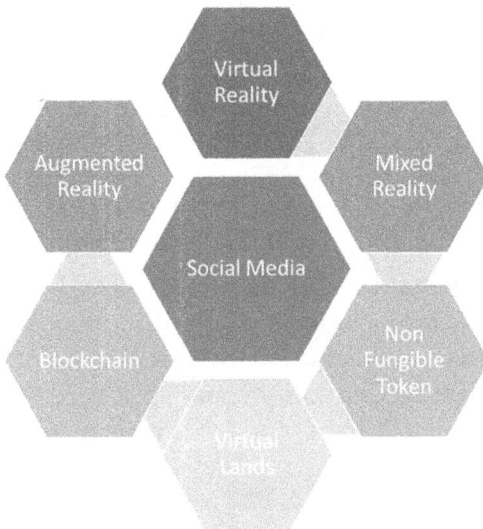

Figure 6 - Current Day Technological Development

Over the last twenty years, we have witnessed the creation of technological components, as seen in Figure 6, making possible the metaverse. Metaverse has now become the convergence of reality and virtual life. Blockchain technology has allowed the rise of virtual assets, with cryptocurrency, i.e. NFT, as the medium of trading and exchange.

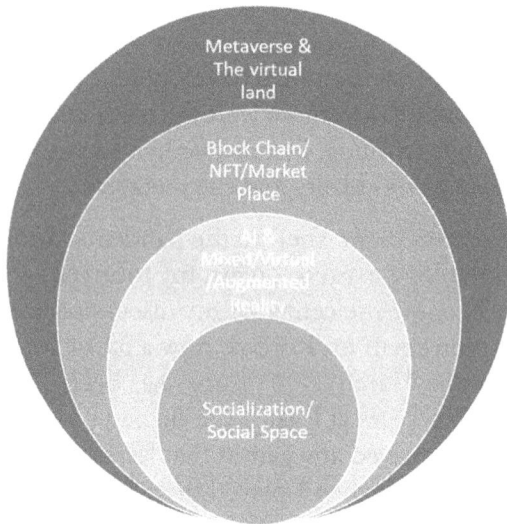

The metaverse, Figure 7, has unified the technological components, community, marketplace, and all in one virtual space, where people can work, play, relax, transact, and socialize.

Figure 7 - Future- The Metaverse

A report presented by JP Morgan in 2021 shows the potential annual transaction value of US$54 billion consumption of virtual goods, primarily in the spending of buying music. Approximately 60 billion messages are sent daily on Roblox, showing the expansion of the metaverse community. The total potential market opportunity is estimated at over US$1 trillion in yearly revenue in the metaverse itself. Major brands, such as Nike, Walmart, GAP, PWC, Adidas, Atari and many more, are flooding into the metaverse due to the market potential, also known as "Second Life". In 2021, Ariana Grande held a virtual concert in Fortnite and grossed about US$20 million in one night. The concert brought in more revenue than the conventional concert because of the borderless nature and the tapping into the worldwide market with minimal operating expenditure.

SUMMARY: A COMPETITIVE STRATEGY FOR HITMAKER GLOBAL ACADEMY

In the past two years, during the COVID-19 pandemic, Hitmaker Global Academy (**Hitmaker**) has continuously reviewed its competitiveness in the industry. Our reviews consider both the financial and non-financial aspects of the business landscape, including a comprehensive analysis of the external environment and our strategic positioning. We have adopted the **S**trategic **P**osition and **A**ction **E**valuation model (**SPACE**) (Jagiello. Kevin & Jackie, 1984).

The model presents Hitmaker's position and standing in four SPACE dimensions: Financial Strength, Competitive Advantage, Industry Attractiveness, and Environment Stability. Hitmaker has chosen SPACE as it recognises the importance of relevance in the industry and the nature of the macro business environment, evaluating the competitive strategy of the company based on the financial and non-financial capability.

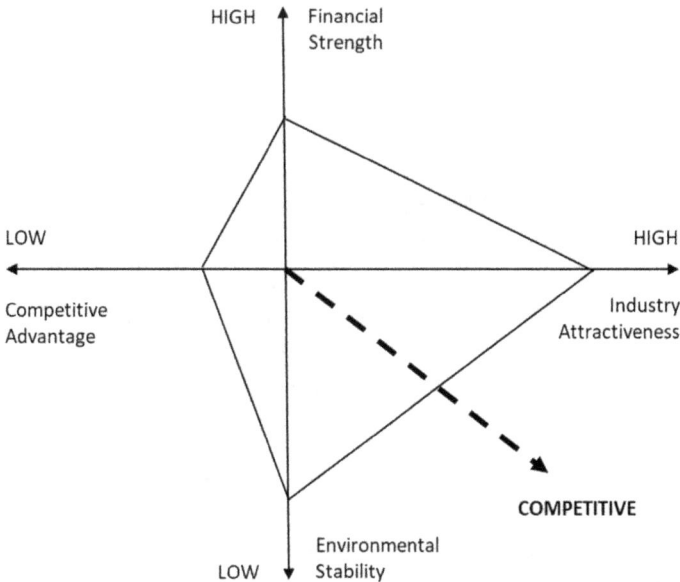

Figure 8 - Hitmaker Global Academy SPACE Model

The SPACE model evaluates the company using a point system to score against a list of key assessment criteria/key imperatives in relation to the four SPACE dimensions. The table below shows the standing of a six-point scale for each dimension of the SPACE model. Each dimension has been assessed thoroughly by the management to ensure:

1. The strategic plan and its key success factors are relevant to the external environment
2. The company considers its financial capability, including key resources to support its strategic plan

External Dimension		
Industry Attractiveness	1 Very Poor	6 Very Attractive
Environmental Stability	-6 Very Unstable/ Hostile	-1 Very Stable/ Supportive
Internal Dimensions		
Financial Strength	1 Very Weak	6 Very Strong
Competitive Advantage	-6 Very Disadvantaged	-1 Very Advantaged

Figure 9 - SPACE Six-Point Score Scale Described

From the analysis, Hitmaker's Competitive SPACE posture arises when the company has a competitive advantage (**-2**) in an attractive industry (**5**) but is held back by low financial strength (**3**) and faces an unstable environment (**-5**). Without the financial strength to build on its position or to buffer itself from environmental hostilities, a competitive/reactionary stance is advocated. The strategic imperatives would be to maintain position whilst improving financial strength and reducing exposure to environmental threats before moving to a more aggressive posture.

This article's beginning shows that businesses are prone to natural and business environment volatility. Nevertheless, we should constantly review the business strategy to remain relevant and strategize to sustain the endless challenges ahead. Hitmaker uses the SPACE model to stay informed of our current position and competitive stance in the competitive arena. As Singapore is currently easing its COVID-19 restrictions, we predict a positive change in the industry is imminent. Post-COVID, Hitmaker shall plan to re-build its strategic posture to the SPACE aggressive strategic thrust, potentially looking at the development of technological advancement with a focus on virtual property and assets in the long-term or, indeed, venturing into the metaverse education space. Hitmaker needs to increase its financial strength to support its strategy to expand its capability in order to compete to gain its market share in the industry, especially in the music and music education scene.

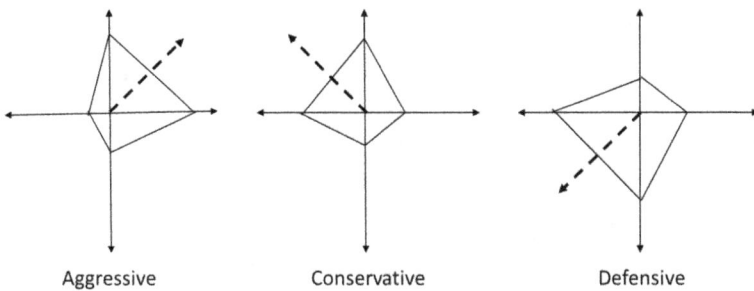

| Aggressive | Conservative | Defensive |

Figure 10 - Other SPACE postures

What is your organisation's post-COVID SPACE posture?

Andy Wong - Co-founder and Executive Director of Hitmaker Global Academy, Singapore. He holds an MBA from the University of Manchester UK and is a Fellow of the UBSS Centre for Scholarship and Research

REFERENCES

Beiner, et. all (2009). *Greatest killer of the twentieth century_ the Great Flu of 1918–19*. 20th Century Social Perspectives, 20th-Century / Contemporary History. *https://www.historyireland.com/greatest-killer-of-the-twentieth-century-the-great-flu-of-1918-19/* [assessed by 01.02.2022]

CB Insights. (2021). *25 Industries & Technologies That Will Shape The Post-Virus World. https://www.cbinsights.com/reports/CB-Insights_Industries-Tech-Shaping-World-Post-Covid.pdf* [assessed by 31.01.2022]

Cheng, A. (Euromonitor). (2016). *Emerging Eyewear Retailing Concepts In Asia Pacific.*

Jagiello, J., Jahiello, K. (2015) Advanced Strategic Management. Manchester Business School. University of Manchester: Manchester. United Kingdom.

JP Morgan. (2022). *Opportunities in the metaverse. https://www.jpmorgan.com/content/dam/jpm/treasury-services/documents/opportunities-in-the-metaverse.pdf* [assessed by 31.01.2022]

Chapter

22

Recovery of Live Music Industry – Imperative for Future of Tertiary Music Institutions in Australia

Jamie Rigg and Ian Bofinger

INTRODUCTION

The impact of COVID-19 in 2020 and 2021 resulted in disastrous years for the live music industry in Australia. Langford (2021) reported that live music attendance suffered a 67.5% decline nationwide between 2019 and 2020, with just 7.7 million tickets sold in 2020, compared to over 23 million tickets in 2019, causing the Australian live music industry to lose $1.4 billion in 2020.

The implications of this economic downturn in the sector have impacted on the desire for students to follow their passion into tertiary music studies that may not have the long-term financial security of other university studies. The choice of studying music at a tertiary level has historically been a concern for parents and students alike, and the impact of the past two years has put further pressure on providers. Some, like the James Morrison Academy at Mount Gambier, have been forced to close in 2022. If the live music industry fails to recover in 2022, there may be other providers that suffer the same fate.

This paper identifies some of the music industry trends that have emerged since the pandemic lockdown that may change the landscape of the Australian Live Music sector and, in turn, reinvigorate the tertiary music sector.

OBSERVATION 1 - MILLENNIALS WILL DRIVE DEMAND FOR GIGS

It is not yet known the extent to which continued COVID restrictions in Australia will affect tours and live concert events through 2022. Current indications show that there is still a market demand, particularly within the millennial generation, who will attend concerts (13 per cent), live music sessions (10 per cent), festivals (9 per cent) and - more than other age demographics - livestream shows (6 per cent).

A 2021 Deloitte study found that Millennials and Gen Zs believe in their individual power to drive change. Respondents to the study indicated that they are focusing their energies upon meaningful action - increasing political involvement, aligning spending and career choices with their values, and driving change on societal issues that matter most to them.

Millennials, who are Australia's largest generation by population, are currently in their earning prime. With the majority of this generation now in the workforce, they now account for a large proportion of Australia's consumer spending. Harris' (2019) research of Millennials reveals this generation not only highly values experiences, but they are increasingly spending time and money on them: from concerts and social events to athletic pursuits, to cultural experiences and events of all kinds.

The combination of this generation's interest in events, and their increasing ability to spend, is driving the growth of the experience economy.

OBSERVATION 2 - THE RETURN OF THE LIVE MUSIC IN THE CORNER PUB

State governments and councils are designing incentives to entice people back to the CBDs, but the Australian live sector maintains consequences of the two-year lockdown will continue and gigs are operating a little differently. As of early 2022, audiences must be seated, vaccination status must be checked, and fewer tickets can be sold because of the one person per four square metres rule.

Whitson and Lannin (2021) report that the music industry was in for a tough summer and would not get back on its feet until at least the middle of 2022. The industry is already estimated to have lost 36,000 jobs since the pandemic hit. As Dean Ormiston, CEO APRA AMCOS, further notes, "Our industry was the first to fall off a cliff with airlines and hospitality last year, but we've got to wait till pubs and clubs are back operating at full capacity before, economically, it works for live music. Patrons rediscovered the significant role music venues played in the community during the lockdowns."

OBSERVATION 3 – EVOLVING WAYS TO FIND NEW EMERGING ARTISTS AND MUSIC

Research has shown that Australians under the age of 30 will increasingly find new music through video games. It's something games developers are aware of, admitting they start sourcing new music a year before a game's release.

Bruce (2022) states that 24% of respondents were already finding new music in games, a figure expected to rise considerably in the next 12 months. 50% of the 18-29 demographic find new music through Apple Music or Spotify (compared to 37% of the general US public), 45% from social media (32% of general public) and one-third from movies and TV shows. 35% of all age groups still get new music from radio (FM, digital and streamed), 31% from recommendations, 14% from ads, 11% from blogs/websites, and 8% from podcasts.

OBSERVATION 4 – ACCESS TO FREE CONTENT

The pandemic has left most Australians stranded at home and turning to their screens to keep themselves entertained. Advertisers, however, have seen their budgets cut or paused as sales continue to plunge. YouGov's 'International media consumption report 2021: Is there a new normal?' white paper examines Australians' generational attitudes towards paid content.

As outlined in Ho (2021), although personal data and privacy concerns have become a growing concern, almost one in five (19%) agree that they are willing to give up their personal data for free content. Men are more willing compared to women (22% vs. 15%). Over half (55%) are willing, and the remaining quarter (24%) are undecided.

The data also shows that attitudes towards exchanging personal data for free content is generational. While over one in five (22%) Gen Z-ers are happy to give away their data, this drops to one in ten (11%) amongst Baby Boomers and less than one in ten (8%) from the Silent Generation. Millennials are the most willing, with a quarter (25%) agreeing they have no issue giving up personal data for free content.

OBSERVATION 5 - NFTS WILL BECOME MAINSTREAM

Some would insist non-fungible tokens (NFTs) are just a fad or, even worse, a sham, but all indications show that having become a US$58 billion market in 2021, with buyers totalling between 10,000 to 20,000 since March, many people believe it's going to go more mainstream. NFTs can really be anything digital, but a lot of the current excitement is around using the tech to sell digital art, such as videos, drawings, and music.

As Clark (2021) explains, at a very high level, most NFTs are part of the Ethereum blockchain. Ethereum is a cryptocurrency, like Bitcoin or Dogecoin, but its blockchain also supports these NFTs which store extra information that makes them work differently from, say, an ETH coin. It is worth noting that other blockchains can implement their own versions of NFTs.

NFTs have a feature that you can enable that will pay artists a percentage every time the NFT is sold or changes hands, making sure that if your work gains popularity and increases in value, the original artists see some of that benefit.

Australia is listed as the ninth most NFT-interested nation - based on Google searches - behind China, Singapore, and Venezuela who top the list. Industry players expect regulations covering NFTs to be introduced in 2022.

OBSERVATION 6 - HIGHER CONCERT PRICES

Ticket prices were already clambering up before COVID, as promoters experimented with tiered payments - to not only take advantage of Australian audiences' penchant for paying top money for concerts, but also to see it as a solution to scalping. According to Live Performance Australia, in 2018, the average ticket price was $99.03 (from $90.59 the year before), while Victorians were charged more at $107.08 per person.

One of the reasons for the greater rise in prices is that promoters are being forced to offer huge fees to road crews and production staff as many have left the industry in the past two years. These staff members have since moved to more traditional jobs which offer regular incomes and normal hours. When they're offered contracts to return for tours and festivals, there is now a demand to be met - how many hours they're guaranteed and what compensation they'll get if there's a cancellation. McKinsey & Company (2020) state, "It's a Catch 22, they won't come back until the live sector's back and the live sector won't be back until they return."

Other costs are rising fuel prices, escalating insurance premiums, additional costs for health authorities to attend, and paying for cancellation refunds.

It is unfortunate that an increase in pricing may deter some patrons from attending, but for others it may also make the live performance experience even more significant and special.

OBSERVATION 7 - TIKTOK WILL GROW

Research suggests TikTok will reach between 1.5 billion and 2 billion monthly users, after a 59.8 per cent growth in 2020, and a 40.8 per cent uptick in 2021. It reached one billion worldwide in September 2021, while the last Australian figure was 2.5 million in early 2020, with monthly usage at 16.8 hours.

This could be interpreted as an ambiguous trend for future development of the Australian Performing Arts Industry, as on the one hand, the platform seems to promote the replication of art, but on the other hand, it can be seen as an avenue for artists to reach a new, wider audience.

OBSERVATION 8 - SONGS WILL BECOME MORE "UPBEAT AND COLOURFUL"

One of the consequences of COVID lockdown was faster and more positive pop songs, something which will continue in 2022. The trend began two years ago. In 2020, the Top 20 songs' average tempo was 122 beats per minute, the highest since 2009.

Artists and audiences alike who faced the bleakness of lockdown are now looking at life's positives. It is most unusual that a children's musical group wins the Triple J network's annual Hottest 100. This occurred on January 22, 2022 and it was The Wiggles' rendition of Tame Impala's "Elephant" that came out on top, ahead of The Kid LAROI and Justin Bieber's "Stay" and Spacey Jane's "Lots of Nothing", respectively.

A McKinsey & Company (2022) report on Covid-19 business implications notes, "There's been some really unusual benefits to COVID. Everyone slowed down for a second and smelled the roses, the Earth breathed for a time, people took stock of what they really appreciated together and fell in love all over."

OBSERVATION 9 - DOGS TO SNIFF OUT MORE THAN DRUGS AT EVENTS

In 2022, sniffer dogs won't be just working at live events to check for drugs, they're also going to be there to detect for COVID. This routine began in the US late 2021 at performances by Metallica, Tool, The Black Keys and Eric Church, after it was discovered that people with COVID have a distinct smell - the dogs are trained to signal their handlers if they detect the virus.

A company overseeing this is Bio-Detection K9 and is headed by Jerry Johnson who worked with dog teams in Iraq and Afghanistan in the 2000s. Johnson is quoted in Rolling Stone (2021), "If you understand the instincts of a dog's behaviour, it makes a lot of sense. Dogs sniff each other to see if that other dog has a virus…We're training them to look for something they'd be interested in anyway."

OBSERVATION 10 – THE MUSIC INDUSTRY IS RESILIENT

The following is a selection of reflections from some prominent Australian-based artists as we move out of the pandemic and seek to breathe new life into the music industry. As Taylor (2022) reports -

Leo Sayer:

(Leo needs no introduction really, you know songs. "You Make Me Feel Like Dancing", "When I Need You", "More Than I Can Say", "Thunder in My Heart", and the list goes on.)

"The creative brain will always have a need to express. Either through art, music or whatever.

The need to write songs was banging on my ear, I couldn't think of anything else I needed to do more. It's been my way of working through this time."

James Morrison:

(Australia's virtuoso multi- instrumentalist jazz superstar)

"We're here to make music and play music and not the instrument. When we teach people music we tend to say, 'I like to work on the feel first and then let the technicalities follow.'

During the pandemic without the gigs, I haven't been playing as much. For as long I can remember, I've taken the trumpet from the case to do gigs, so it was difficult for me to just practise. Luckily, when I did my first gig out of lockdown, I found I was able to play as I had pre lockdown.

I put this down to the stamina I had developed as a younger musician.

So much of what we are as musicians is in our heads."

Darryl Beaton:

(Darryl Beaton is a multi-instrumentalist and musical director for the likes of Jessica Mauboy, Delta Goodrem, Guy Sebastian, Katie Noonan and Stan Walker.)

"This is just the nature of the music industry, you have to weather the storm - it's the jungle we live in. There will always be good and bad times. Luckily, I've found that I could generate an income through song writing and playing on other artists' tracks."

Jade MacRae:

(Jade MacRae was born into a life of music. Her mother (Joy Yates - vocals) and father (Dave MacRae - piano) are both exceptional musicians and artists in their own right, having toured and recorded with the likes of Van Morrison, Cat Stevens, Gladys Knight, Elvin Jones, Clark Terry, The Buddy Rich Big Band, Chet Baker, Scott Walker, Allan Holdsworth and countless others.)

"My vision for the next 12 months is to reconnect, establish myself as a soul artist in my own right and get back into the position of performing my own music in quality venues. I was privileged to have had a great music education and to be mentored by some fabulous musicians and that is what I hope for the next generation of young emerging musicians."

One final observation

The testimonials of these artists display a commonality, in that, mentoring, education and experience have helped to guide their careers and made it possible for them to survive the pandemic.

There are indications of a 2022 rebirth of live music in Australia, but as this paper identifies, to achieve this some things may never be the same.

Adjunct Professor Jamie Rigg is an accomplished musician, arranger, producer, and music educator. He is also a Fellow of the UBSS Centre for Entrepreneurship.

Professor Ian Bofinger is the Executive Dean and CEO of AMPA, the Australian Academy of Music and Performing Arts. He is also a Fellow of the UBSS Centre for Scholarship and Research.

REFERENCES

Browne, D. (2022) Who Let the Dogs In? Covid-Sniffing Canines Are Helping Keep Metallica, Eric Church on the Road
https://www.rollingstone.com/music/music-news/covid-sniffing-dogs-concert-tours-1280953/

Bruce, G (2022) How are global consumers finding new music?
https://yougov.co.uk/topics/technology/articles-reports/2022/01/04/how-are-global-consumers-finding-new-music

Clarke, M (2021) NFTs, explained - I have questions about this emerging... um... art form? Platform?
https://www.theverge.com/22310188/nft-explainer-what-is-blockchain-crypto-art-faq

Deloitte (2021) Global 2021 Millennial and Gen Z Survey
https://www2.deloitte.com/global/en/pages/about-deloitte/articles/millennialsurvey.html

Ho, K. (2021) A Quarter of Australian Millennials Willing to Exchange Personal Data for Free Content
https://au.yougov.com/news/2021/02/26/quarter-australian-millennials-willing-exchange-pe/

Live Performance Australia LPA 2019 and 2020 Ticket Attendance and Revenue Report *https://reports.liveperformance.com.au/ticket-survey-2019-2020/#/*

McKinsey & Company (2022) COVID-19: Implications for Business *https://www.mckinsey.com/business-functions/risk-and-resilience/our-insights/covid-19-implications-for-business*

McKinsey & Company (2020) The path to the next normal Leading with resolve through the coronavirus pandemic
https://www.mckinsey.com/~/media/McKinsey/Featured%20Insights/Navigating%20the%20coronavirus%20crisis%20collected%20works/Path-to-the-next-normal-collection.pdf

Taylor, S (2022) The Gig Life Podcast
https://www.thegiglifepodcast.com

Whitson, R and Lannin, S (2021) Live music bouncing back as COVID-19 lockdowns end, but damage is lasting
https://www.abc.net.au/news/2021-10-19/music-covid-lockdown-live-holy-holy-clypso-tours-festivals/100527110

Compilation of References

Reference	Ch
Abrahams, F. (2005). The application of critical pedagogy to music teaching and learning. Visions of Research in Music Education, 6.	4
Adorno, T.W. (2000, January). On popular music. Soundscapes. *https://www.icce.rug.nl/~soundscapes/DATABASES/SWA/On_popular_music_1.shtml*	4
Aesop. 620 - 564 BCE. Aesop's Fables	8
AICD *https://aicd.companydirectors.com.au/-/media/cd2/resources/director-resources/director-tools/2019/board/07236-4-13-board-minutes-fa.ashx#:~:text=There%20are%20no%20requirements%20under,requisitioned%20in%20a%20court%20action*	5
American Bar Association. 2019. Robotic Automation Can Improve Your Practice. 01 07. Accessed 01 20, 2022. *https://www.americanbar.org/groups/law_practice/publications/law_practice_magazine/2019/JA2019/JA19PerySimon/*	8
Anderson, C., 2004. *https://miloszkrasinski.com/the-long-tail-effect-theory-in-practise-explained/*	12
Ang, P., & Kiew, C. (2020, June 16). *Artists defend value of creative work to society after survey sparks debate.* The Straits Times. *https://www.straitstimes.com/lifestyle/arts/artists-defend-value-of-creative-work-to-society-after-survey-sparks-debate*	16
Antley (2020) *https://www.webce.com/news/2020/07/16/professional-development#:~:text=The%20purpose%20of%20professional%20development%20is%20to%20give%20professionals%20the,knowledge%20base%20for%20your%20field*	7
ASIC *https://asic.gov.au/for-business/registering-a-company/steps-to-register-a-company/constitution-and-replaceable-rules/*	5
ASIC *https://asic.gov.au/regulatory-resources/corporate-governance/shareholder-engagement/faqs-virtual-meetings-for-companies-and-registered-schemes-held-on-or-before-31-march-2022/* accessed 30 December 2021	5
Australasian College of Pharmacy *https://www.acp.edu.au/*	7
Australian Broadcasting Corporation. 2018. Fact check: Has the rate of casualisation in the workforce remained steady for the last 20 years? 17 04. Accessed 01 20, 2020. *https://www.abc.net.au/news/2018-04-17/fact-check-casualisation/9654334*	8
Australian Pharmacy Council *https://www.pharmacycouncil.org.au/*	7

Reference	Ch
Baker J (2021) Sydney University pursues hybrid model of online and in-person classes, December 1, 2021. *https://www.smh.com.au/national/nsw/sydney-university-pursues-hybrid-model-of-online-and-in-person-classes-20211201-p59duj.html*, viewed December 10, 2021.	2
BANK, W. (2021, October. *https://www.worldbank.org/*. Retrieved from *https://www.worldbank.org/en/country/indonesia/overview#1*	18
Bean M and Dawkins P (2021) Review of University-Industry Collaboration in Teaching and Learning. *https://www.dese.gov.au/higher-education-reviews-and-consultations/resources/universityindustry-collaboration-teaching-and-learning-review*	2
Beiner, et. all (2009). *Greatest killer of the twentieth century_ the Great Flu of 1918–19.* 20th Century Social Perspectives, 20th-Century / Contemporary History. *https://www.historyireland.com/greatest-killer-of-the-twentieth-century-the-great-flu-of-1918-19/* [assessed by 01.02.2022]	21
Benham, S. (2003). Being the other adapting to life in a culturally diverse classroom. Journal of Music Teacher Education, 13(1), 21-32	4
Blakey, C. & Major, C. 2019, 'Student Perceptions of Engagement in Online Course: An Exploratory Study', Online Journal of Distance Learning Administration, vol. XXII, no. 4., *https://www.westga.edu/~distance/ojdla/winter224/blakeymajor224.html*	19
Botstein, L. (2019). *The future of music in America: The challenge of the COVID-19 pandemic.* The Musical Quarterly, 102(4). 351-360. *https://doi-org.ezproxy.bu.edu/10.1093/musqtl/gdaa007*	16
Bradley C, Hirt M, Hudson S, Northcote N and Smit S (2020) The Great Acceleration. *https://www.mckinsey.com/business-functions/strategy-and-corporate-finance/our-insights/the-great-acceleration*, viewed April 2, 2021.	2
Browne, D. (2022) Who Let the Dogs In? Covid-Sniffing Canines Are Helping Keep Metallica, Eric Church on the Road *https://www.rollingstone.com/music/music-news/covid-sniffing-dogs-concert-tours-1280953/*	22
Bruce, G (2022) How are global consumers finding new music? *https://yougov.co.uk/topics/technology/articles-reports/2022/01/04/how-are-global-consumers-finding-new-music*	22
Business Advice UK (2019) *https://businessadvice.co.uk/business-development/the-benefits-of-professional-development/*	7
CB Insights. (2021). *25 Industries & Technologies That Will Shape The Post-Virus World. https://www.cbinsights.com/reports/CB-Insights_Industries-Tech-Shaping-World-Post-Covid.pdf* [assessed by 31.01.2022]	21

Reference	Ch
Cheng, A. (Euromonitor). (2016). *Emerging Eyewear Retailing Concepts In Asia Pacific.*	21
Chris (2016) *https://www.josephchris.com/10-benefits-of-professional-development*	7
Chugunov. (2021), *Macro Stability and Economic Growth*. ECONOMICS, T. (2021). https://tradingeconomics.com. Retrieved from *https://tradingeconomics.com/thailand/interest-rateGROUP*	18
Clarke, M (2021) NFTs, explained - I have questions about this emerging... um... art form? Platform? *https://www.theverge.com/22310188/nft-explainer-what-is-blockchain-crypto-art-faq*	22
Conner. (1993). Managing At the Speed of Change. Random House. Retrieved from *https://www.amazon.com/Managing-Speed-Change-Daryl-Conner/dp/0679406840*	3
Courtenay, W. 1980. "The Effect of the Black Death on English Higher Education." Speculum 55: 696-714. *http://www.jstor.org/stable/2847661*	6
Crawford (2016) *https://www.bizjournals.com/bizjournals/how-to/growth-strategies/2016/09/professional-development-matters-success-company.html#:~:text=Professional%20development%20helps%20employees%20continue,but%20also%20excel%20in%20it.&text=Actively%20pursuing%20professional%20development%20ensures,and%20directions%20in%20an%20industry*	7
Deloitte (2021) Global 2021 Millennial and Gen Z Survey *https://www2.deloitte.com/global/en/pages/about-deloitte/articles/millennialsurvey.html*	22
Dillon, D., 2017. NewcastleStudio. *http://www.newscaststudio.com/2017/09/20/production-music-now-billion-dollar-industry*	12
Egan, P. 2020 The Black Death and an Educational Renaissance, *https://educationalrenaissance.com/2020/04/03/the-black-death-and-an-educational-renaissance/*	6
Fatemi, F. (2022, January 24). *Here's how NFTs could define the future of music*. Forbes. *https://www.forbes.com/sites/falonfatemi/2022/01/24/nfts-and-the-future-of-music/*	16
Freire, P. (1970). Pedagogy of the oppressed. New York, NY: Continuum.	4
Friday, C. 2021 *University Disruption Will Continue Beyond COVID-19* *https://www.ey.com/en_au/covid-19/university-disruption-will-continue-beyond-covid-19*	17
Friesen, N., 2012. Defining blended learning. Learning Spaces. *https://www.normfriesen.info/papers/Defining_Blended_Learning_NF.pdf*	19

Reference	Ch
Gallagher M (2001) E- Learning in Post-Secondary Education: Trends, Issues and Policy Challenges Ahead, 7th OECD/Japan Seminar, June 5 and 6, 2001.	2
Gay, G. (2000). Culturally responsive teaching: Theory, research, and practice. New York: Teachers College Press	4
Gay, G. (2002). Preparing for Culturally Responsive Teaching. Journal of Teacher Education, 53(2), 106-16	4
Gibson W (1984) Neuromancer, Ace, New York, USA.	2
Gibson W (1993) Fresh Air Radio Interview, National Public Radio (August 31, 1993).	2
Graham, C. R. (2006). Blended learning systems: Definition, current trends, and future directions. In C. J. Bonk & C. R. Graham (Eds.), The handbook of blended learning: Global perspectives, local designs (pp. 3-21). San Francisco: Pfeiffer.	19
Gu, X., Domer, N., & O'Connor, J. (2021). *The next normal: Chinese indie music in a post-COVID China.* Cultural Trends, 30(1). 63-74. *https://doi.org/10.1080/09548963.2020.1846122*	16
Gumuchian, M-L. (2021, March 23). *Music soothes pandemic blues as 2020 record sales hit a high note.* Reuters. *https://www.reuters.com/article/us-music-sales-ifpi-idUSKBN2BF22F*	16
Half (2017) *https://www.roberthalf.com/blog/management-tips/professional-development-training-a-win-for-the-entire-team*	7
Hall, H., & Davison, B. (2007). Social software as support in hybrid learning environment: The value of the blog as a tool for reflective learning and peer support. *https://www.napier.ac.uk/~/media/worktribe/output-238428/social-software-as-support-in-hybrid-learning-environments-the-value-of-the-blog-as-a.pdf*	19
Handy, Charles. 1989. The Age of Unreason.	8
Harvard Business Review. 2020. Remote Managers Are Having Trust Issues. 30 07. Accessed 01 20, 2022. *https://hbr.org/2020/07/remote-managers-are-having-trust-issues*	8
Harvard Business Review. 2021. Who Is Driving the Great Resignation? 15 09. Accessed 01 20, 2022. *https://hbr.org/2021/09/who-is-driving-the-great-resignation*	8
Hawke, A. 2022 *Australia welcomes return of international students and backpackers https://minister.homeaffairs.gov.au/AlexHawke/Pages/australia-welcomes-return-of-international-students-and-backpackers.aspx*	17
Hein, G.E. (1991). Constructivist learning theory. Exploratorium. *https://www.exploratorium.edu/education/ifi/constructivist-learning*	4

Reference	Ch
Higher Education Educator, 2021 *Australia NSW to welcome back some international students https://www.theeducatoronline.com/k12/news/nsw-to-welcome-back-some-international-students/278777*	17
Ho, K. (2021) A Quarter of Australian Millennials Willing to Exchange Personal Data for Free Content *https://au.yougov.com/news/2021/02/26/quarter-australian-millennials-willing-exchange-pe/*	22
Hogan S (2021) Virtual reality a "positive impact" on hybrid learning, posted on Nov 11, 2021. *https://thepienews.com/news/vr-positive-impact-hybrid-model-learning/*, viewed December 15, 2021.	2
Holon IQ (2021b) 109 New OPM Bootcamp and Pathways Partnerships in Q1, 2021. *https://www.holoniq.com/notes/100-new-opm-bootcamp-and-pathway-partnerships-in-q1-2021/*, viewed December 10, 2021.	2
HolonIQ (2021a) 244 University Partnerships in the First Half of 2021. *https://www.holoniq.com/notes/opm-mooc-opx.-244-university-partnerships-in-the-first-half-of-2021/*, viewed September 24, 2021.	2
https://www.mckinsey.com/featured-insights/future-of-work/from-surviving-to-thriving-reimagining-the-post-covid-19-return Accessed 27/01/2022	11
https://www.weforum.org/agenda/2020/11/transform-business-model-post-covid-future/ Accessed 27/01/2022	11
Huss, J. A., Sela, O., & Eastep, S. (2015). A case study of online instructors and their quest for greater interactivity in their courses: Overcoming the distance in distance education. Australian Journal of Teacher Education, 40(4): 72-86 *http://dx.doi.org/10.14221/ajte.2015v40n4.5*	4
Jackson, C. 2022 *'Looking down the barrel': Australian universities face nervous future post-Covid https://www.theguardian.com/australia-news/2022/jan/30/looking-down-the-barrel-australian-universities-face-nervous-future-post-covid*	17
Jagiello, J., Jahiello, K. (2015) Advanced Strategic Management. Manchester Business School. University of Manchester: Manchester. United Kingdom.	21
Jankoff, C and Bendel, D (2020) "Business War Stories from the Trenches" Smart Questions	11
Jankoff, C and Bendel, D (2021) "What can we learn from Everyday successful Australian entrepreneurs?" Smart Questions	11
JHU CSSE COVID-19 Data *https://www.nsw.gov.au/covid-19*	17
Jick. (1993). Managing Change: Cases and Concepts: Text and Cases. McGraw-Hill. Retrieved from *https://www.amazon.com.au/Managing-Change-Cases-Concepts-Text/dp/0073102741*	3

Reference	Ch
Johnson, V.M. (2008). Learning as a social process. Veronica Johnson.	4
Johnson. (1999). Who Moved My Cheese. Vermilion. Retrieved from *https://www.amazon.com.au/Moved-Cheese-Spencer-M-D-Johnson/dp/0091816971/*	3
Jonathan Dingel, Brent Neiman. 2020. How Many Jobs Can Be Done at Home? 06 04. Accessed 01 20, 2022. *https://papers.ssrn.com/sol3/papers.cfm?abstract_id=3569412*	8
JP Morgan. (2022). *Opportunities in the metaverse.* *https://www.jpmorgan.com/content/dam/jpm/treasury-services/documents/opportunities-in-the-metaverse.pdf* [assessed by 31.01.2022]	21
Kanwar, Anurag *https://www.ubss.edu.au/articles/2021/may/online-teaching-a-tale-of-two-institutions/* accessed 30 December 2021	5
Kaplan Solution (2021) *https://www.kaplansolutions.com/article/5-benefits-of-professional-development*	7
Kidd, E. (2020) 'My staff don't want to return to work - coming back after COVID-19'. Human Resources Director, 12 May 2020	1
King, A. (1993). From sage on the stage to guide on the side. College Teaching, 41(1), 30-35. Kruse, A. J. (2016). 'They wasn't makin' my kinda music': A hip-hop musician's perspective on school, schooling, and school music. Music Education Research, 18(3), 240-253. *https://doi.org/10.1080/14613808.2015.1060954*	4
Kotter. (1996). Leading Change. Harvard Business Review Press. Retrieved from *https://www.amazon.com.au/Leading-Change-New-Preface-Author/dp/1422186431*	3
LaMarsh. (1995). Changing the Way We Change. Prentice Hall. Retrieved from *https://www.amazon.com.au/Changing-Way-Change-Jeanenne-Lamarsh/dp/0201633647*	3
Lasalle College of the Arts. (2021, May 15). In Wikipedia. *https://en.wikipedia.org/wiki/LASALLE_College_of_the_Arts*	4
Live Performance Australia LPA 2019 and 2020 Ticket Attendance and Revenue Report *https://reports.liveperformance.com.au/ticket-survey-2019-2020/#/*	22
Lumsden, Andrew *https://aicd.companydirectors.com.au/resources/covid-19/virtual-member-meetings* accessed 4 January 2022	5
Margolies D. and Strub J. (2021) 'Music Community, Improvisation, and Social Technologies in COVID-Era Música Huasteca'. Frontiers in Psychology. 31 May 2021.	14

Reference	Ch
McIssac, M. S., Blocher, J. M., Mahes, V., & Vrasidas, C. (1999). Student and teacher perception of interaction in online computer-mediated communication. Educational Media International, 36,121-131	4
McKinsey & Company (2020) The path to the next normal Leading with resolve through the coronavirus pandemic *https://www.mckinsey.com/~/media/McKinsey/Featured%20Insights/Navigating%20the%20coronavirus%20crisis%20collected%20works/Path-to-the-next-normal-collection.pdf*	22
McKinsey & Company (2022) COVID-19: Implications for Business *https://www.mckinsey.com/business-functions/risk-and-resilience/our-insights/covid-19-implications-for-business*	22
McLuhan, M 1964. Understanding Media: The Extensions of Man, Signet Books, New York.	6
Micallef and Kayyali (2019) *https://scholar.google.com.au/scholar_url?url=https://www.mdpi.com/2226-4787/7/4/154/pdf&hl=en&sa=X&ei=KzPrYbWLKIqL6rQP9ZGweA&scisig=AAGBfm2teAcliBKTNS_aGLnbm5eM26hEMg&oi=scholarr*	7
Mirroshnikov, G. (2021). Education's Hybrid Future: What We Know from Research. *https://campustechnology.com/articles/2021/07/21/educations-hybrid-future-what-we-know-from-research.aspx*	19
Mizierska E. and Rigg T. (2021) 'Challenges to British Nightclubs During and After the Covid-19 Pandemic'. Dancecult: Journal of Electronic Dance Music Culture. 14 December 2021.	14
Motherwell, S. (2022) *Here's who can enter WA after February 5 and what they need to do after arriving https://www.abc.net.au/news/2022-01-21/wa-hard-border-restrictions-approved-traveller-list/100772308*	17
News, V. N. (2021) *https://vietnamnews.vn/* Retrieved from *https://vietnamnews.vn/economy/592363/covid-19-highlights-need-for-economic-restructuring.html*	18
Ng, J. S. (2021, June 6). *Singaporean music conductor who became a delivery rider due to Covid-19 gets advisory role in arts charity.* Today Online. *https://www.todayonline.com/singapore/singaporean-music-conductor-who-became-delivery-rider-due-covid-19-gets-advisory-role-arts*	16
Nicholas, A.J. (2020). Preferred learning methods of generation Z. Salve Regina University. *https://digitalcommons.salve.edu/cgi/viewcontent.cgi?article=1075&context=fac_staff_pub*	4
Niska. 2022. Niska Retail Robotics. 20 01. Accessed 01 20, 2022. *https://niska.com.au/*	8

Reference	Ch
Noonan P (2019) Review of the Australian Qualifications Framework Final Report 2019. *https://www.dese.gov.au/download/4707/review-australian-qualifications-framework-final-report-2019/18863/document/pdf*, viewed May 10, 2021.	2
O'Connor, T. 2021. VCE in China: a case study, in "Exploring a New Era: Hybrid, Blended and Online Learning" (ed.) Whateley, G., West, A. and Chanda A. UBSS publication. *https://www.ubss.edu.au/ubss-reports/?tab=Reports%202016%20-2022*	6
OECD. (2020). The Impact Of Covid-19 On Education Insights From Education At A Glance 2020. Retrieved from *https://www.oecd.org/education/the-impact-of-covid-19-on-education-insights-education-at-a-glance-2020.pdf*	3
Onderdijk K. et al. (2021) 'Livestream Experiments: The Role of COVID-19, Agency, Presence, and Social Context in Facilitating Social Connectedness'. Frontiers in Psychology. 24 May 2021.	14
Phillips, A, 2021. My distributor list can be found using the territorial flags on this menu here. *https://101.audio/distributors/*	12
Phillips, A, 2021. 101's releases can be viewed and heard as marketing teasers at *https://101.audio/releases/*	12
Phillips, A, 2021. As I quote to my students: *'Effective entrepreneurs are exceptional learners'*, UBSS Entrepreneurship Research Report, lecture, May 2021	12
Price, D. (2019). Constructivism as a theory for teaching and learning. Simply psychology. *https://www.simplypsychology.org/Zone-of-Proximal-Development.html*	4
Price, D. (2019). The zone of proximal development and scaffolding. Simply psychology. *https://www.simplypsychology.org/constructivism.html*	4
Professionals Australia *http://www.professionalsaustralia.org.au/australian-government/blog/the-importance-of-continuing-professional-development/*	7
Regelski, T. A. (2005). Curriculum: Implication of aesthetic versus praxial philosophies. In D.J. Elliott (Ed.) Praxial music education: Reflections and dialogues. (pp. 219-248). Oxford University Press. *https://doi.org/10.1093/acprof:oso/9780195385076.003.12*	4
Regelski, T.A. (2002). On "methodolatry" and music teaching as "critical" and reflective praxis. In Philosophy of Music Education Review, 10(2): 102-104.	4
Rinchakorn. (2022). *https://www.gotoknow.org/posts/484062*	18
Roy, A. (2021, December 28). *The music industry in the metaverse: re-energized revenue streams*. XRToday. *https://www.xrtoday.com/virtual-reality/the-music-industry-in-the-metaverse-re-energised-revenue-streams/*	16

Reference	Ch
Sankey M (2021) Australasian Council on Open, Distance and eLearning (ACODE), Returning to lectures in 2021. *https://www.acode.edu.au/pluginfile.php/9235/mod_resource/content/7/white%20paper.pdf*	2
Saw, C., Lin, J., & Jie, W. Y. (2020). *Economic Survey of Singapore First Quarter 2020. Impact of the COVID-19 Pandemic on the Singapore Economy.*	18
Schwab K (2017) The Fourth Industrial Revolution, Penguin UK, Great Britain.	2
Senge, P. (1990). The Fifth Discipline: The Art & Practice of The Learning Organization. Crown. Retrieved from *https://www.amazon.com.au/Fifth-Discipline-Practice-Learning-Organization/dp/0385517254/*	3
Sisario, B. (2021, May 2). *Musicians say streaming doesn't pay. Can the industry change?* The New York Times. *https://www.nytimes.com/2021/05/07/arts/music/streaming-music-payments.html*	16
Skordis, W., Haghparast, H., Batura, N., Hughes, J. (2015). Learning online: A case study exploring student perceptions and experience of a course in economic evaluation. International Journal of Teaching and Learning in Higher Education, 27(3): 413-422.	4
Steinbuch, Y. (2021, February 10). Professor realizes end of 2-hours Zoom lecture that he was on mute. New York Post. *https://nypost.com/2021/02/10/professor-in-singapore-on-mute-for-entire-two-hour-lecture/*	4
Suwannasopon, T. (2021, November 30). *Economics MCR001. Vietnam economics: Monetary and future trend after Covid-19.*	18
Swanson, K. (2013). *A case study on Spotify: exploring perceptions of the music streaming service.* Music & Entertainment Industry Educators Association Journal, 13 (1). 207–230. *https://doi.org/10.25101/13.10*	16
Taylor, A. (2021, February 8). How Covid is 'creating' a new genre for live music. BBC. *https://www.bbc.com/news/entertainment-arts-55947209*	4
Taylor, S (2022) The Gig Life Podcast *https://www.thegiglifepodcast.com*	22
TEQSA (2021b) Forward impact of COVID-19 on Australian higher education. *https://www.teqsa.gov.au/latest-news/publications/forward-impact-covid-19-australian-higher-education-report*, viewed December 15, 2021.	2
TEQSA (2021b) Undergraduate Certificates Continue until Mid-2025. *https://www.teqsa.gov.au/latest-news/articles/undergraduate-certificates-continue-until-mid-2025*, viewed December 15, 2021.	2

Reference	Ch
The Irish Times. (2020, April 3). 'Lagging wifi, internet freezes, distractions': Students on the reality of online classes. The Irish Times. *https://www.irishtimes.com/news/education/lagging-wifi-internet-freezes-distractions-students-on-the-reality-of-online-classes-1.4220198*	4
TIMES, T. B. (2021). *https://www.businesstimes.com.sg/hub/*. Retrieved from *https://www.businesstimes.com.sg/hub/indonesia-76th-independence-day/indonesian-governments-strategies-in-response-to-covid-19*	18
Universities Australia (2021) Australia's Migration Program 2022-2023. *https://www.universitiesaustralia.edu.au/wp-content/uploads/2021/12/211213-Australias-Migration-Program-2022-2023-Submission.pdf*	2
UNSW. 2021. Future of Work Literature Review: Emerging trends and issues. 09. Accessed 01 20, 2022. *https://www.unsw.adfa.edu.au/sites/default/files/documents/Future_of_Work_Literature_Review.pdf*	8
Vandenberg F., Berghman M., and Schaap J. (2020) 'The 'Lonely Raver': Music Livestreams during COVID-19 as a Hotline to Collective Consciousness?' European Societies. 14 September 2020.	14
Vogado, S. (2021). *https://www.focus-economics.com/*. Retrieved from *https://www.focus-economics.com/countries/thailand/news/fiscal/government-announces-mildly-expansionary-fy-2021-budget-amid-ongoing*	18
W. B. (2020). *COVID-19 Policy Response Notes of Vietnam*. Ho, G. (2020). *https://www.straitstimes.com*. Retrieved from *https://www.straitstimes.com/singapore/government-mounting-fiscal-firepower-fighting-covid-19-number-one-job-dpm-heng*	18
Washington Post. 2021. Transcript: The Great Resignation with Molly M. Anderson, Anthony C. Klotz, PhD & Elaine Welteroth. 24 09. Accessed 01 20, 2022. *https://www.washingtonpost.com/washington-post-live/2021/09/24/transcript-great-resignation-with-molly-m-anderson-anthony-c-klotz-phd-elaine-welteroth/*	8
West (2021) *https://www.ubss.edu.au/media/2716/what-is-meant-by-blended-learning.pdf*	7
West A (2021) OPM is not just another TLA, Chapter 14, Updating and enhancing unit content, delivery, and assessment (Hooke and Whateley). *https://www.ubss.edu.au/articles/2021/october/opm-is-not-just-another-tla/*	2
West A and Whateley G (2021) 'The fourth industrial age is here for higher education to embrace' was published on Monday, May 10 in Campus Review.	2
Whateley G., West A. and Chanda A (2021) Exploring a new era – hybrid, blended and online learning. Smart Questions, ISBN 978-1-907453-31-1.	2

Reference	Ch
Whateley, G. (2021) 'What is meant by 'hybrid' delivery and how does it work in higher education'. Campus Review, 12 July 2021	1
Whateley, G. (2021). What is meant by 'hybrid' delivery and how does it work in higher education? *https://www.ubss.edu.au/media/2670/understanding-hybrid-delivery.pdf*	19
Whateley, Greg *https://www.ubss.edu.au/article/the-impact-of-a-pandemic-on-the-approach-to-management-and-change/* accessed 4 January 2022	5
Whitson, R and Lannin, S (2021) Live music bouncing back as COVID-19 lockdowns end, but damage is lasting *https://www.abc.net.au/news/2021-10-19/music-covid-lockdown-live-holy-holy-clypso-tours-festivals/100527110*	22
World Economic Forum. 2021. What is 'The Great Resignation'? 29 Nov. Accessed 01 20, 2022. *https://www.weforum.org/agenda/2021/11/what-is-the-great-resignation-and-what-can-we-learn-from-it/*	8
Wu, A. M. (2021, June). *https://www.csc.gov.sg/*. Retrieved from *https://www.csc.gov.sg/articles/fiscal-responses-to-covid-19-in-singapore-and-hong-kong*	18
Yamungkoon,O.N. (2021). *Comparison of four ASEAN countries GDP, during Covid-19, 2019-2021*	18
Zaglas, W. (2020) 'Delivering quality feedback to students and staff with remote learning and skeleton staff'. Campus Review, 11 September 2020	1

List of Figures

Notes pages

We hope that this book has inspired you and that you have already scribbled your thoughts all over it. However, if you have ideas that need a little more space then please use these notes pages.

www.ingramcontent.com/pod-product-compliance
Lightning Source LLC
Chambersburg PA
CBHW070444100426
42812CB00004B/1205